THE

Word of Promise

THE
Word of Promise

A HANDBOOK
TO THE
Promises of Scripture

BY
HORATIUS BONAR, D.D.

"All the promises of God in him are yea, and in him Amen." — 2 Cor. i. 20.

First Published 1850
First Ambassador Productions Edition 1986

AMBASSADOR PRODUCTIONS LTD
241 Upper Newtownards Road,
Belfast BT4 3JF.

455 Great Western Road
Glasgow G12 8HH.

Printed in the United Kingdom by
Ambassador Productions Ltd.

ISBN 0 907927 09 2

PREFACE

The following work does not profess to exhaust the subject indicated by its title. It is means rather as a *selection* than a *collection* of Divine words of promise. It is not meant as a mere book of reference — a dictionary of the promises, but is designed to be thoroughly readable.

In the earlier sections the extracted passages are briefly given, in order not unduly to swell the work. This, however, it is hoped, will only have the effect of leading to a careful consultation of the context for fuller light and significance. In some of the latter sections, such as "Israel," it was found impossible to be so compact and concise, the nature of the promise compelling the quotation of something beyond a clause or a verse, and the continuity of the passage demanding the paragraph or chapter in full.

The earlier sections and sub-sections are prefaced with remarks bearing on the subject which the subsequent passages point to. The latter ones are not all thus introduced; it being desirable in a general work like the present to avoid a defined and detailed indication of prophetical views; the words of Scripture being thus left to speak for themselves.

In these days of Handbooks, this handbook of the promises may be found of service to the church of God.

ROMAN NUMERALS
— Conversion —

$$i = 1$$
$$v = 5$$
$$x = 10$$
$$l = 50$$
$$c = 100$$

The letters composing a number are ranged in order of value and the number meant is found by addition.

If a letter or a set of letters is placed before a letter of higher value it is to be subtracted from it before the addition is done.

CONTENTS.

PART I.

THE WORD OF PROMISE.

CHAPTER I.

PART II.

THE PROMISES.

CHAPTER I.

FOR THE SINNER.

vi   *Contents.*

CHAPTER II.

FOR THE SAINT.

Contents.

CHAPTER III.

FOR THE CHURCH.

Contents.

CHAPTER IV.

FOR ISRAEL.

Contents.

CHAPTER V.

FOR THE WORLD.

CHAPTER VI.

FOR SPECIAL CASES AND PERSONS.

PART I.

———◆———

THE WORD OF PROMISE

CHAPTER I.

THE SURENESS OF THE WORD.

WE enter on this field by asking attention to a few thoughts as to the true nature of a promise, and as to the word on which every promise rests.

In all promises God is speaking to us as only God can speak ; he speaks in truth and love ; he expects to be credited and trusted. Let us not wrong him by suspicion or coldness. Let us do justice to his word and to himself.

" The word of promise," says Owen, " is the soul's great supportment in waiting for God ;" and another has truly said that " every promise is built upon four pillars :—God's justice or holiness, which will not suffer him to deceive ; his grace or goodness, which will not suffer him to forget ; his truth, which will not suffer him to change ; and his power, which makes him able to accomplish."

A *promise* is something sent on beforehand to tell of something else coming after. It is from a Latin word meaning " foresent ;" a *foresent* word, or sign, or deed, making sure to us something better than itself, which must be waited for.

The faint light-streaks in the east are the promises of day, foresent to tell us that the sun is coming up in his strength. The seed is the promise of the flower ; and the spring-bud is the promise of autumn with its mellow fruit.

It is the will of God that binds together past and present and future ; and in the promise we have the intimation of that will. We trust the future because of the present and the past. The thing that hath been is that which shall be, and that which is done is that which shall be done.

He who sends the messenger, or gives the sign, or speaks the word, is the promiser; and it is on his character for truthfulness that we depend in regard to the certainty of that which is to come. If he be faithless, or rash in promising, or unable to carry out his own will, or vacillating in his purposes, his messages are worthless. They are hollow sounds that do but mock us ; worm-eaten planks flung across a stream, which look like a bridge, but are too frail to be trusted even by a child. If, however, he be true and powerful, and stable in purpose, then the thing to come is as sure as that which has come. His promise is the substance of things hoped for, the evidence of things not seen. For every thing that gives worth to a promise depends on the truth and grace and power of the promiser; and as in Scripture we have to do with Him who is not a man that he should lie, nor the son of man that he should repent, we are sure that not one good thing shall fail which he has forespoken.

A promise does indeed sometimes seem to fail. It sounded well, but it has passed away, and nothing has come forth from it. It shot up, but it has died down; its root seems to have become rottenness, and its blossom to have gone up as dust. So was it with the first promise regarding the woman's seed, which lay dormant for four thousand years; and not till then came to pass the saying that is written, "Behold, a virgin ('*the* virgin,' it should run) shall conceive, and bear a son." But the temporary failure is the permanent success; the promise departs for a season that it should be realized for ever. Like the corn of wheat, it falls into the ground and dies, in order that it may not remain alone, but be more fruitful. Through death it is, we may say, that many a promise passes to resurrection, and that which was sown in weakness is raised in power. To many a troubled spirit, forecasting sorrowfully its own future, or the world's future, or the

Church's future (as if the link had snapped, and the truth of God failed), we may say, "That which thou sowest is not quickened except it die." Many are the promises which, like the stars, are hidden by light, and need darkness to bring out their lustre—

> "Like secret characters,
> Invisible till opened to the light,
> Or like the potter's paintings, colourless,
> Till they have passed to glory through the flames."

"He ever wins that sides with God," it has been well said; and we may add, he ever wins who trusts in God, and gives him credit for speaking truthfully, for meaning what he says, and for an unfailing purpose to carry out every jot and tittle of what he has declared. To be in sympathy with God as to the present, rejoicing that his will is done, and that it is just what it is—this is one side or phase of faith, producing healthy tranquillity of soul. To trust him with the future, because it is his future, and because we are to be partakers of that future with him according to his word of promise—this is the other side of faith; and fitted not only to make us "careful for nothing," but to "rejoice in hope," to look into the cloudiest future that ever hung over a Church or an age, with serene though solemn eye.

It is not a little remarkable that in the Hebrew there is no special term for promise. That which our version renders "promise" is simply "word;" yes, WORD, no more. God's word is his promise. With men more may be needed, "and an oath for confirmation is to them the end of all strife;" but with God this is not required. With one so true, so loving, so powerful, so unchangeable, a word is enough. He speaks, and it is done.

It is even more remarkable that the Hebrew term for *word* is the same as for *deed*. God's words are deeds. "I have pronounced the word," says he (Jer. xxxiv. 5). "I will hasten my word to perform it" (Jer. i. 12). "None of my words shall be prolonged" (Ezek. xii. 28). "The days are at hand, and *the effect* (literally 'the word') of every vision" (Ezek. xii. 23). "Then came the word of the Lord, saying, Is there *any thing* (literally 'any *word*') too hard for me?" (Jer. xxxii. 26, 27.) With God, to speak the thing is to do it; the word uttered from his almighty lips would have done the thing at the very moment, had not he for a season restrained its power and interposed an interval between the utterance and the consummation. Volition, and speech, and action among men are very different things, quite separable from each other, nay, at variance

sometimes with each other; but it is not so
with God. When he says a thing it is as
good as done; and you may call it either
a word, or a thing, or a fact. With him a
promise is not a messenger sent on before to
tell of something to be done; it is itself the
fulfiller and performer. With him the interval
between the saying and the doing is as
nothing; the promise contains the thing; the
word conveys the deed; the declaration carries
in its own bosom its fulfilment and execution.
"Let there be light," he said, "and there was
light;" for he commanded the light to shine
out of darkness; he spoke creation out of
nothing; for "where the word of a king is, there
is power" (Eccles. viii. 4). By his word all
things have been, are, and shall be; by the
word of God the heavens were of old; and he
who is called "The WORD of God" is repre-
sented as "upholding all things by the word of
his power" (Heb. i. 3). Yes; "his word runneth
very swiftly" (Ps. cxlvii. 15); and yet it hardly
seems to overtake his doings; like the two
disciples, word and deed "run both of them
together."

These true sayings of God which we call
his "promises," but which he, more simply,
calls his "words," are of various kinds, and
spoken to many classes. Let us arrange

these, and we shall find in such an arrangement not a mere matter of convenience, but a help to the right understanding of the passages. The true location of a text is often in itself an interpretation.

It is of great use to place the sayings of God in different lights, and to look at them on all sides.

No doubt the place in which the Holy Spirit has set them is their true one, and the best. Their position in Scripture, like that of the stars in the firmament, is not by chance, nor according to the wisdom and will of man, but of God.

But it is useful, often needful, to take them out of their place, either to study them by themselves or in other connections. This change of position and relation is often of much service to us, without being an injury or a dishonour to the word. How excellent and perfect must that book be which can bear to be thus taken to pieces and to have its fragments exhibited in such a variety of aspects! No human work could bear to be thus handled without suffering loss. Only that which is Divine loses not, but rather gains by each such subdivision and dismemberment, each new collocation and cross-reflection. For thus is the beauty, the fitness, the radiance of each part brought out on all sides and in all lights ; and the splendour of the fragments is found to be as marvellous as the perfection of the whole.

He who has wandered through Galilee, knows the striking variety of aspects in which Mount Tabor shows itself from each new point of view.   At a distance it looks simply a part of the hills of Zebulun, a little higher than the rest, like a watch-tower, overlooking the great plain on one side, and the Sea of Tiberias on the other.   But as you come nearer it seems to stand alone in majesty.   As you take one side and another, and another, it changes its shape and colour ; now breaking off from one of its fellow hills, now linking itself to another ; now in light, now in shade ; now barely clad, now rich with wooded verdure ; now an erect cone, now an overturned and flattened one ; yet amid all these changes, beautiful.   So he who travels through Scripture will find its words to be.   Whether separate or united, whether set in this relation or in that, whether studied on one side or another, each saying is goodly, and will stand the scrutiny of all positions and all eyes ; nay, it courts these ; asks to be turned round and round like a well-cut diamond with a hundred facets, in order that its lustre may be fully seen.

This, I may say, is one of the most striking tests of inspiration. Each verse, each word can stand this peculiar scrutiny, without revealing any imperfection or flaw. You may dislocate and disarrange its parts, thus altering its aspect and form; but, somehow or other, this only brings new perfections to light, and each fresh fracture exhibits some new beauty. What book could bear such handling whose words were not Divine?

To say that there is inspiration in the *book*, but not in the *words*, is to use a formula which will not bear analysis. For of what is the book composed? Of thoughts. And how do these thoughts reach us? Through words, the words which we read in this volume; for there is no other way. If the thoughts are perfect, but the words imperfect, how is it possible for us to extract the truth? If both thoughts and words are imperfect, the difficulty of reaching the truth is greatly augmented; nay, rises into impossibility. The truth that is in the Bible must remain undiscovered and undiscoverable if the formula in which it is embodied be inaccurate or even doubtful; for inaccuracy of language must be absolutely fatal to the discovery of truth. The certainty of doctrine cannot rise above the certainty of the language in which it is

communicated. If I know that the words of
the first chapter of St. John are not true and
correct, or if I cannot be sure that they are
true and correct, the information which I derive from that portion of Scripture has neither
proof nor resting-place. The wisdom I gather
from it may be of a higher kind than Plato's,
but it carries no authority, no certainty; for
the words are but the words of John the
fisherman, an unlettered man, for the accuracy
of whose diction we have no security, save on
the one admission, that he wrote as he was
moved by the Holy Ghost. It is not likely
that the Galilean fisherman could have expressed his own thoughts correctly; *it is certain that he could not, unaided, have expressed
the thoughts of God.* For who can write the
thoughts of God but God himself, especially
when the language in which they are to be
written is not that of heaven but of earth, the
poor, cramped language of fallen humanity,
*in which rightly to utter the things of God
would be a transcendent miracle?* A first-rate
musician might perhaps draw harmony out of
the strings of a broken harp, an unskilful one
could not. He that is so incredulous of the
supernatural as to wish to strike the miracle
of inspiration out of its words is only showing
himself one of the most credulous of men;

denying the lofty miracle of God giving forth his thoughts in words of his own Divine selection, yet adopting the absurd miracle of an unlettered Jew expressing in adequate diction truth which he himself barely comprehended, wisdom the depth of which he had never fathomed.

To deny the Divine origin and accuracy of the words of Scripture is to take away the only explanation of the existence of that book at all, to create useless miracles, and to destroy the possibility of reaching certainty in the things of God.

It is reckoned philosophical to say that inspiration is in the Bible, but not in its words; or to say that it contains the history of an inspired people, but is not an inspired book. To us this seems but a cowardly infidelity, veiling itself in the language of mysticism; or if not infidelity, it is certainly fanaticism, and fanaticism of a very unmeaning kind; for let men say what they will, the expression that inspiration is in the Bible though not in its words, when subjected to analysis, means either that we have no inspired Bible at all, or no Bible so pervaded with the mind of God as is "Paradise Lost" with the mind of Milton; no Bible that can be called the Book of God in half so true a sense as the "Novum Organum" can be called the Book of Bacon.

Confidence, then, in the perfection of Scripture and in the Divine accuracy of its words, must be the foundation of any treatise on its promises. For how idle to select, or classify, or comment on sentences, of the accuracy of which you are not sure, and for whose authority as an infallible utterance you feel that you have no evidence. Of what avail would it be for me to press home upon any fellow-man such words as, "He will abundantly pardon," or, "Seek ye me, and ye shall live," if I cannot tell him that these are the very words of God himself; not a thought of God embodied, perhaps very imperfectly, in man's words, but the very utterance of God, the words of his lips, and the outflowing of his heart?

Without this confidence, the link between the promise and the promiser is broken; for I cannot know whether the former truly represents the mind of the latter; and unless I know this, a promise is a mockery. If the gracious words which I read truly represent the gracious speaker, and are exact revelations of his mind and heart, then I rejoice in them. They are honest as well as loving words; authentic expositions of a grace which I feel to be altogether suitable. But if the words are defective, ambiguous, and only very indirectly Divine, then I am, in so far as security is concerned, without a promise ; for I can only feel secure if I am absolutely persuaded that the words I rest on are the words of the living God. Nothing else will bear my weight. Faith cannot fasten itself to a human anchor ; it cannot build on any foundation less than Divine. It believes, because it knows that God has spoken. It stands not in feeling, or intuition, or senti-ment, or speculation, but in the genuine word. Anything less than this is sand, not rock. " Faith cometh by hearing, and hear-ing by the word of God " (Rom. x. 17).

The whole comfort of a promise depends upon its being the very word of the Promiser, the revelation of God's mind to us. Take away this and its pleasant sound is nothing but a sentiment, or a soothing verse of poetry, or a cheering melody. It speaks with no authority, and can be no real help. It can heal no wounds, open no prison doors, ad-minister no medicine, strengthen no weak-ness, nerve us against no adversary, lead us on to no victory. It can only say peace when there is no peace ; not pacifying the conscience, but only lulling it asleep ; working on our spiritual constitution only as an opiate which dulls our senses while it relieves our pain, and sets us upon imagining that we are not what we are.

The Bible promises all land us in God himself; and each word is a round in that Divine ladder whose foot is at our door, and whose top rests against the gate of the heavenly city.

Each promise is, more or less, a gospel; speaking good news from God, "the God of all grace:" how absolutely indispensable, then, that each word be true, be Divine; nay, be certainly known as such. If there be uncertainty as to the words, there must be uncertainty as to all the grace that they may contain; for we derive all our knowledge of the grace from the words in which it is declared. If the words fail us, the ground on which we stand gives way; we are cheated, we are mocked, a deception has been practised upon us, the aspect of gladness which the promise presented to us vanishes away.

Let me call the promises the title-deeds of my inheritance. Each clause in these is of importance to me; for on it my right to this or that portion of the heritage will rest. Each word in each clause is of no less moment; for on the true meaning of it the construction of the clause, nay, the scope and bearing of the whole Testament, may turn. If, then, I have but a sketch of that will, and that sketch drawn out by a person, it may be of honest intentions, but of very inferior mind to the testator, and not capable of entering into his feelings and purposes, I have no security for anything which that title-deed contains, for I have no evidence that one word in it, from first to last, is the testator's own. It may embody his views with substantial correctness, but law disregards all such " substantial accuracy," where the words are not present to verify it ; for all law insists on having the words of such documents before it, and on interpreting these words for itself.

So is it with the heart, so is it with the conscience in receiving the promises of Scripture. They insist on knowing the accuracy, the Divine accuracy, of the words which affect them. They cannot be content with the vague idea of a "substantial accuracy," or a general inspiration ; they insist on taking up the very words and interpreting each ; and though something very much short of Divine accuracy would satisfy the mere intellect or judgment, especially in cases where no great interests or possessions are concerned, yet this, and nothing less than this,

do the heart and conscience demand, in
matters of infinite concern, when once
awakened to the importance of the transac-
tions between the soul and God. " Substantial
accuracy" and "general inspiration," may
serve as long as the question of the soul's
eternal welfare is not stirred in earnest. But
let the man get beyond theological specula-
tions, beyond theories, beyond the niceties of
metaphysics ; let him be roused up and
brought face to face with a just God ; let him
be confronted with the alternative of heaven
or hell, then he must be certified as to the
thorough accuracy of the Bible declarations
of grace. He must be certified that such
words as grace, and mercy, and love, and
pardon, and justification, and blood, and
sacrifice, and atonement, and reconciliation,
and all such, are Divine, not human words;
words which God has himself attested as
expressing his very mind ; words, on the
Divine accuracy of which he has given the
man to understand that he may confidently
rest ; words which he tells him to take up and
plead with him ; words out of which the heart
may lawfully extract Divine consolation, and
the conscience Divine peace.

Ah, when a man ceases to trifle with
eternity; when he becomes in earnest about

his immortal welfare, the thorough inspiration of Scripture becomes an absolute necessity. The Divine accuracy of the words which contain the truth on which he must rest for eternity, is indispensable. Between a fully inspired Bible and no Bible at all he sees no alternative. A half-inspired Bible (if such a thing can be) may do for one half in earnest, but nothing less than a wholly-inspired Bible will do for one wholly in earnest. Before he awoke he might speculate and trifle with the Book and its contents ; now he decides he cannot halt between two opinions any longer. His soul is in peril ; his inheritance is at stake ; he must ascertain whether he can trust to his title-deeds, and whether he may venture to call each word accurate, and to risk his eternity upon each declaration and promise, as altogether true and Divine.

He who has come to the conclusion that Scripture is but partially inspired, must feel that he has got a very imperfect and unsatisfactory book. If he be an honest truthseeker, he must have reached this conclusion with a sorrowful heart ; for, on the most vital of all subjects, he has got a most unsafe guide and teacher ; one to whose tuition he cannot commit himself implicitly, and whose statements he must always accept with large allowance, or rather with positive distrust.

If a man be an admirer of Socrates, he regrets deeply that he has none of the actual writings of that philosopher to study. He consoles himself, indeed, with the thought that he has the sentiments of Socrates preserved by his pupils, Xenophon and Plato. Still he grieves that he has no treatise directly from his pen; and, noble as are the "Memorabilia" of the one pupil, and the "Dialogues" of the other, he feels that he has got Socrates only at second-hand; he has got only what his disciples thought he held or said, without the means of verifying the accuracy of their report, or ascertaining from the words of the great Athenian himself whether they were right or wrong. If any issue of importance hangs on his knowing and believing the opinions of Socrates, that issue has become an impossibility, seeing his words have perished. To know what Socrates believed, I must know what he said. His two admirers have done their work well, and sketched their master's views perhaps more eloquently than he himself could have done; but, as they do not profess to report his very words, they have left us an imperfect work, out of which no examination, however searching, can produce satisfactory results. For as in searching the words of a man in order to discover his sentiments, the deeper and more minute our search is, the likelier we are to arrive at the truth ; so in searching the words of a man in order to discover the sentiments, not of himself, but of another whose opinions he is stating, the more minute our investigations are into the words, the more uncertain they become, leading us perhaps entirely out of the proper track, and revealing to us simply the views and guesses of a reporter.

If such be the case when the author we are studying is Socrates, and his reporter is Plato, how much more when that author is God himself, and his reporters the untaught fishermen of Galilee ? If Plato's "Dialogues," however beautiful, be necessarily defective, and incapable of being founded on for any exact information as to the theories of the master, simply because the words are not vouched for as those of Socrates, how much more defective and untrustworthy must our first Gospel be, if we find in it only the words of Matthew the publican—Matthew the publican attempting to delineate in his own language the character of Christ, and to represent, according to his own perception of them, the infinite truths of God ? We may trust Plato, perhaps, as giving us very closely the mind of Socrates; but shall we trust Matthew for giving us with that accuracy which in such matters is absolutely indispensable, the very mind of God?

It is, then, through the words of the Promiser that we find our way into his mind and heart. We know what he thinks, what he feels, what he purposes, by what he has spoken. The glory of a promise lies not simply in its Divine origin, but in its being a revelation of God himself to us. It is not so much a declaration, or a pledge, or an assurance of love, as a fragment of that love itself. Of himself the Lord has said, "Believest thou not that I am in the Father, and the Father in me? he that hath seen me hath seen the Father." So of each heavenly promise we may truly say the same.

If any, then, say to us, "Show us the Father, and it sufficeth," we take them to the gracious word, and tell them he is there. You may know what he is and how he feels by what he speaks, by what he promises. For he has given us "exceeding great and precious promises: that by these we might be partakers of the Divine nature, having escaped the corruption that is in the world through lust" (2 Pet. i. 4).

In these words of promise there is no exaggeration, no mistake, and no delusion. They are all strictly true. They are not random sayings, nor words of course. We need not be afraid to put too kind a construction upon them, as if God could mean less than he says. He may mean more, but he cannot mean less; for in his words, as much as in his doings, he is "a God of TRUTH and without iniquity, just and right is he." The Divine truthfulness is too little remembered by us. "The Strength of Israel will not lie" (1 Sam. xv. 29); nor does he cause any one "to trust in a lie;" his anointing is truth and is no lie (1 John ii. 27); and the darkest crime of man is that of not believing God's record, and so making him a liar (1 John v. 10).

As the Son of God is the gift of the Father (John iv. 10), so the Holy Spirit is specially the promise of the Father (Luke xxiv. 49). He is both the gift of God (Acts viii. 20) and the promise of God (Acts i. 4). In him are all promises summed up, and he who has the Holy Spirit has every promise of God. The Spirit is both the thing promised and the Promiser. He has written them all; and he speaks to us out of them all. In the promises we come most directly into contact with the Holy Ghost. It is "the love of the Spirit" (Rom. xv. 30) that breathes and burns

through all of them. When his words abide
in us, then he himself abides in us ; for it is
of an indwelling Spirit that the Bible speaks ;
and it is his indwelling love and word that
gladden and purify the soul.

As the promises are thus connected with
the Holy Spirit, so are they also with Christ.
"All the promises of God in him are yea,
and in him Amen, unto the glory of God by
us" (2 Cor. i. 20). More fully, though not so
concisely, may these words be rendered,
"Whatsoever, or how many soever, be the
promises of God, in him is the yea, and in
him the Amen, for glory to God through
us ;" that is, in him is the verification and
confirmation of them all ; he is their Alpha
and their Omega, their centre and circum-
ference, their certainty, and truth, and fulness.
Without Christ, what would a promise be ?
With him, what is there that it does not
contain ? As God, on the fourth day,
gathered up the wide-scattered beams of
light and deposited them in the central sun,
so did he bring together the scattered promises of Scripture and treasure them up in
Christ, constituting him at once their pledge,
their earnest, and their fulfilment. We see
them in him and him in them ; all their excellency centered and revealed in him, and

all his excellency radiating from them in many-coloured brightness.

To reason concerning anything in this way, " God has promised it, therefore he will give it," as if we trusted God simply because he was committed to the fulfilment of the promise and could not draw back, is to take but a narrow and one-sided view of the case. No, we may trust him if he has promised; but is the promise, after all, the real ground of our confidence? Does not our confidence in the promise arise from our knowledge of Him from whose lips it has come? God is true, and God is love, must ever be the basis of our trust. It is a blessed thing to have so many of his gracious words; but what are these if separated from himself? Take them as so many legal deeds which we could enforce by law, and they are barren as well as cold. Take them as the utterances of full-hearted affection, and they are warm and blessed, even though we were persuaded that we could not lay legal claim to the fulfilment of one of them.

Thus the brightest thing about the promises is that they are the revelation of God himself, the exhibition of the manifold grace that is in him. It is this view of them that disposes of the question so often put by the troubled heart, "Is this promise for *me?*" We may not be always able to satisfy ourselves that such and such words point to us personally; but if they shed new light on the gracious character of that God with whom we have to do, they do more than solve our doubts; for they take us into an inner region of grace, and show us something beyond a promise, "the exceeding riches of the grace of God."

When we light upon some Old Testament promise, we sometimes fear to touch it. We look upon it as a gem belonging to another. We say, "Ah, that is for Israel, not for the Gentile, not for the sinner, not for the Church, not for me." Perhaps it is for Israel; but what of that? Do we need to rob Israel in order to get it for ourselves? No; there is a more excellent way, by means of which we may extract and enjoy all the blessing, and yet leave Israel's share in it unrifled and un- touched. All that God says to Israel illus- trates his character as "the God of all grace," and it is upon this character that we rest our faith. Every word that reveals more of God and his love to us, strengthens our faith and elevates our joy. It is this that makes the first promise so precious, and it is this that gives fulness and power to all subsequent words of promise. The promise given to our first parents in Paradise was, in one view, very general. Adam's posterity might have misgivings as to its direct bearing on themselves; and if their consolation was to come from some special personality in the promise which might embolden them to say, it was meant individually for me, they would have remained uncomforted. But the glory of the promise was its revelation of the grace of God, and its proclamation of the coming Christ, the woman's seed. He to whom a promise has shed brightness on the character of God, has been enriched thereby. He who has learned from a promise (be it to Jew or Gentile, to Israel, or to Egypt, or to Assyria) something of the person and work of Messiah, has learned something which will make him, through the Holy Spirit's power, a wiser and a holier man ; something which will gladden him not only for a lifetime here below, but for an eternity in the kingdom of God.

[For the statements on the inspired accuracy of Scripture language, the writer of this volume alone is responsible. In compiling a work on the Promises, he felt very strongly that the actual value of a promise must be measured by the extent to which the words conveyed the exact mind of God. If the words were inaccurate, the promise was worthless ; or if their accuracy were UNCERTAIN, the promise, to the extent of that uncertainty, became inefficacious AS A PROMISE, however precious might be the general truth which it embodied. This thought led him into the train of remarks which his introductory statements contain ; but to these he alone stands committed.]

CHAPTER II.

THE ARRANGEMENT OF ITS PROMISES.

THE purpose which we have in view in this volume requires that we should classify the promises. Any such classification, in order to be useful, must be comprehensive as to its general subjects, and at the same time minute in its details.

By means of a proper arrangement, such as we refer to, the dislocation of passages, which a book like this to a certain extent implies, will be the less felt. The true meaning will be preserved, even though the natural position be altered. The new connection into which they will thus be brought will illustrate, and not injure; will, by means of the new juxtaposition, cause the words from different parts of Scripture to furnish mutual help and to reflect mutual light. The unartificial distribution of the Bible gems throughout its pages, without regard to classification, serves one purpose; and the selecting and arranging of these, the bringing together the emerald.

or ruby, or sapphire, or amethyst, into one bright heap, will serve another.

I am quite aware that this dislocation or artificial arrangement has, in many cases, produced misinterpretation, as in many others it has been founded upon it. But so far is this evil from being unavoidable, it is that which a good classification of kindred passages would greatly help in preventing. A proper arrangement should assist the right understanding of the word, should form a clue to its true meaning, should be a safeguard against distortion. It should be a commentary, as every fair collocation of parallel texts must be. Instead of taking off the edge of a passage, it adds a keener one; instead of weakening, it strengthens; instead of darkening, it lights up. It isolates and makes prominent certain words which otherwise might be overlooked. It surrounds a text with kindred texts, a truth with kindred truths, for a special purpose; when that purpose has been served, the text and the truth go back to their original places, without injury or distortion. The original connection is not broken by the formation of this temporary connection. The authentic and Divine position which each passage occupies in the Bible is not set aside or treated as an accident by the temporary alteration of that position in order to the better study and appreciation of the promise or the doctrine. This manner of dealing with Scripture is not irreverence, nor favouritism, nor caprice; it founds itself upon the persuasion of the perfection of the word—a perfection so peculiar that these disjunctions, and alterations, and new collocations, only exhibit and enhance it the more.

We propose to arrange these "promises," or "sure words of God," under the following general heads. Promises—

    I. For the Sinner.
    II. For the Saint.
    III. For the Church.
    IV. For Israel.
    V. For the World.
    VI. For Special Cases and Persons.

Under these heads we shall be able to arrange the Bible promises. Sometimes a promise may belong to more than one of these heads. This, however, will produce no confusion; at the most, a little repetition here and there may be the result.

Thus, for the better understanding of some, and for the closer application of others, it will be useful to classify the promises.

Not as if their natural location were not

the best, but, assuming this as undoubted, we may survey them on every side and study them in their varied fragments. It seems impossible to handle them, whether separately or in their authentic connection, without gathering light and profit from them.

Their natural order is not certainly in accordance with man's theories of symmetry or rules of art. When he builds a temple its parts are all elaborately planned, chiselled, polished, set in exact harmony, the one against the other. When God builds his "high places," his Alps or his Andes, he flings the mountains together in groups or heaps, with nothing of that which a human architect would call symmetry or order. And do we not regard this mountainous confusion the very perfection of magnificence? We would not have it otherwise. A world with its heights and valleys set in regular architectural order would be poor and tame. Yet for needful purposes, for the ends of the geographer or geologist, we separate or classify these; we take a rock or peak by itself; we form sections at different parts, or break off fragments, in order to set them in other lights and positions, in order to bring out to view their internal structure and strata.

It is thus that we would, though with

reverent hands, deal with Scripture and its promises; not that we may diminish, but magnify them; not that we may destroy, but develop their beauty and their fulness.

May we not, then, close with the apostle's blessing and prayer? " Grace and peace be multiplied unto you through the knowledge of God, and of Jesus our Lord, according as his Divine power hath given unto us all things that pertain unto life and godliness, through the knowledge of him that hath called us to glory and virtue: whereby are given unto us EXCEEDING GREAT AND PRECIOUS PROMISES : that by these ye might be partakers of the Divine nature, having escaped the corruption that is in the world through lust " (2 Pet. i. 2–4).

PART II.

———◆———

THE PROMISES.

PART II.

THE PROMISES

THE PROMISES.

WE now proceed to the words themselves. They are "words of eternal life;" words containing in them all that we can possibly need during our sojourn here.

They are not barren letters or syllables. "The words that I speak unto you, they are spirit, and they are life" (John vi. 63).

In all of them God really *means* what he says; and by them we are brought into contact, not merely with the thoughts of God, but with God himself. Let the living truth which they contain penetrate our whole being. Let the health of which they are full pervade us. Let them be nourishment and strength to us; the joy of our hearts and the light of our eyes.

We ask attention to the way in which God has spoken of his words of promise.

He calls them " exceeding great and precious promises " (2 Peter i. 4). He speaks of his " holy promise " (Ps. cv. 42); of " his good promise which he has promised " (1 Kings viii. 56); of " the covenants of promise " (Eph. ii. 12); of " his promise in Christ " (Eph. iii. 6);

of "the promise of life in Christ Jesus" (2 Tim. i. 1). He tells us that "he is not slack concerning his promise" (2 Peter iii. 9); he says of himself, "he is faithful that promised" (Heb. x. 23); nay, that he "abideth faithful: he cannot deny himself" (2 Tim. ii. 13). He commends his ancient saints, because they "judged him faithful who had promised" (Heb. xi. 11). He calls the good news "the Gospel of God, which he had promised afore by his prophets in the Holy Scriptures" (Rom. i. 2). Abraham is noted as one who "received the promises" (Heb. xi. 17); and the other saints are spoken of as those who "obtained promises" (Heb. xi. 33); nay, Israel itself as the people "to whom pertaineth the promises" (Rom. ix. 4).

Thus God speaks of his promises; and thus he presents them to us as his true and faithful sayings.

"Having therefore these promises, dearly beloved, let us cleanse ourselves from all filthiness of the flesh and spirit, perfecting holiness in the fear of God" (2 Cor. vii. 1).

To what classes or persons they are spoken we mean to show in the pages that follow.

CHAPTER I.

FOR THE SINNER.

THE promises under this head all rest upon the great fact, that man is undone, totally undone ; not partially, but *wholly* lost ; " under condemnation," " under wrath "

These promises are not to a better class of sinners, nor to those who shall contrive to raise themselves out of their utter ruin. There are none which ask man to meet them *half way*, or which go *half way* to meet him All promises for the sinner go the entire way, and come up to each fallen son of Adam on the spot where he is, and in the condition in which he is. Grace takes nothing for granted but sin and unworthiness.

The promise and the sinner thus meet together as altogether suitable ; mutually intended the one for the other ; the sinner suiting the promise, and the promise suiting the sinner.

In regard to this class of promises, there is a strange difference of treatment and opinion among those to whom they come ; a difference arising from not seeing that it is to them simply *as sinners* that the promise speaks ; and that in such a case the question of greater or less, of better or worse, has no place at all. By not observing this, some have come to consider themselves as too bad for a certain promise, and others as too good; both classes looking at it as not suitable for them; the one wishing it had come down a little lower, the other that it had not come down quite so low. Pride and self-righteousness, working in different ways, lie at the root of both these feelings. The man who says, "I am too bad for that promise," is resting his title to it on goodness or merit, and would fain be a little better, in order to be in circumstances for receiving it. The man who says, "I am too good for that promise," is saying, "I am not quite such a sinner, not quite so destitute of goodness, as that promise supposes ; it may do well enough for publicans and sinners, but it does not exactly suit me."

In both these cases, apparently so opposite there is the same unwillingness to own *the want of goodness* as that which makes the promise suitable; for the question turns not upon *degrees* of good or of evil, but upon its existence at all. He who is a sinner at all will find that he needs the whole promise, and nothing less; he who is the greatest sinner will discover that nothing more is needed. God's free love, embodied in the promise, is that which meets the sinner's case; nothing short of this will do for the better class (if such there be); and nothing more than this is required for the worst.

1. THE THIRSTY.

The natural thirst of man is that uneasiness of the bodily organs which water allays; so the thirst of soul is that feeling of unhappiness which only the living water can remove. The springing of that living water is the forgiving love of God. Man longs to be happy, but knows not how. God meets him with his free love. He himself is the fountain of living water; and of this fountain he asks each sad child of Adam to drink.

"Ho, every one that thirsteth, come ye to the waters" (*Isa.* lv. 1).

"I will pour water upon him that is thirsty, and floods upon the dry ground" (*Isa.* xliv. 3).

"With joy shall ye draw water out of the wells of salvation" (*Isa.* xii. 3).

" If thou knewest the gift of God, and who it is that saith to thee, Give me to drink; thou wouldest have asked of him, and he would have given thee living water " (*John* iv. 10).

" Whosoever drinketh of this water shall thirst again : but whosoever drinketh of the water that I shall give him shall never thirst ; but the water that I shall give him shall be in him a well of water springing up into everlasting life " (*John* iv. 13, 14).

" In the last day, that great day of the feast, Jesus stood and cried, saying, If any man thirst, let him come unto me, and drink. He that believeth on me, as the Scripture hath said, out of his belly shall flow rivers of living water " (*John* vii. 37, 38).

" I will give unto him that is athirst of the fountain of the water of life freely " (*Rev.* xxi. 6).

" Let him that is athirst come. And whosoever will, let him take the water of life freely " (*Rev.* xxii. 17).

" He that believeth on me shall never thirst " (*John* vi. 35).

2. THE HUNGRY.

Who will show us any good ? is the cry of the soul. The sinner is hungry for something that will feed his famished spirit, which has hitherto only fed on ashes or the world's husks. God gives him " bread ; " nay, "the bread of God ; " nay, "the bread of life ; " nay, provides a feast ; nay, "kills for him the fatted calf." There is bread enough and to spare. Men may say to a poor sinner, Go and buy; Jesus says, " They need not depart, give ye them to eat."

" Come, eat of my bread, and drink of the wine which I have mingled " (*Prov.* ix. 5).

" Behold, I have prepared my dinner : my oxen and my fatlings are killed, and all things are ready : come unto the marriage " (*Matt.* xxii. 4).

" Eat ye that which is good, and let your soul delight itself in fatness " (*Isa.* lv. 2).

" Labour not for the meat which perisheth,

but for that meat which endureth unto everlasting life" (*John* vi. 27).

"I am the bread of life: he that cometh to me shall never hunger" (*John* vi. 35).

"Come ye, buy, and eat; yea, come, buy wine and milk without money and without price. Wherefore do ye spend money for that which is not bread?" (*Isa.* lv. 1, 2.)

"I am that bread of life. . . . This is the bread which cometh down from heaven, that a man may eat thereof, and not die" (*John* vi. 48, 50).

"I am the living bread which came down from heaven: if any man eat of this bread, he shall live for ever: and the bread that I will give is my flesh, which I will give for the life of the world" (*John* vi. 51).

"He that eateth of this bread shall live for ever" (*John* vi. 58).

"When he had spent all, there arose a mighty famine in that land; and he began to be in want. And he went and joined himself to a citizen of that country; and he sent him into his fields to feed swine. And he would

fain have filled his belly with the husks that
the swine did eat : and no man gave unto
him. And when he came to himself, he
said, How many hired servants of my father's
have bread enough and to spare, and I perish
with hunger ! I will arise and go to my father
. . . And he arose, and came to his father.
But when he was yet a great way off, his
father saw him, and had compassion, and ran,
and fell on his neck, and kissed him. . . . But
the father said to his servants, . . . bring
hither the fatted calf, and kill it; and let us
eat, and be merry " (*Luke* xv. 14–23).

" He hath filled the hungry with good
things " (*Luke* i. 53).

3. THE WEARY.

Every son of Adam is a weary man. He
labours in the fire and vexes himself for very
vanity. He spends his money for that which
is not bread, and his labour for that which
satisfieth not. Sin, vanity, vexation, dis-
appointment, sorrow,—nay, pleasure, mirth,
gaiety, lust, folly, have wearied him. These
have made him what each sinner finds himself to be, a weary man. He goes about seek-

ing rest and finding none; trying all the proffered resting-places of earth, but finding them vain. How suitable does God's promise of rest seem to him, when he begins to bethink himself! He says—

> "Does the gospel word proclaim
> Rest for those that weary be?
> Then, my soul, put in thy claim,
> Sure that promise speaks to thee.
>
> "Marks of grace I cannot show,
> All polluted are my best,
> Yet I weary am, I know,
> And the weary long for rest."

" This is the rest wherewith ye may cause the weary to rest; and this is the refreshing " (*Isa.* xxviii. 12).

" Stand ye in the ways, and see, and ask for the old paths, where is the good way, and walk therein, and ye shall find rest for your souls " (*Jer.* vi. 16).

" I have satiated the weary soul " (*Jer.* xxxi. 25).

" Come unto me, all ye that labour and are heavy laden, and I will give you rest. Take my yoke upon you, and learn of me; for I am meek and lowly in heart: and ye shall find rest unto your souls" (*Matt.* xi. 28, 29).

"They could not enter in because of unbelief. . . . We which have believed do enter into rest" (*Heb.* iii. 19; iv. 3).

4. THE BLIND.

Having eyes, they see not! Such is every man in his natural estate. He sees the things of earth and the face of man; but he is blind to the things of Heaven and to the face of God. He does not see the cross, nor the blood, nor the mercy-seat. A report of these things comes to his ears, but he heeds it not; for the things themselves have no beauty, no excellence in his eyes. He needs to have his eyes opened and the scales taken off. To such Christ presents himself, as the opener of the eyes of the blind, as the possessor of the heavenly eye-salve, one touch of which makes the eyes of the blindest to see. To the blind the promise comes.

"Anoint thine eyes with eye-salve, that thou mayest see (*Rev.* iii. 18).

"The Lord openeth the eyes of the blind" (*Ps.* cxlvi. 8).

" The eyes of the blind shall see out of obscurity, and out of darkness" (*Isa.* xxix. 18).

" The eyes of the blind shall be opened " (*Isa.* xxxv. 5).

" I the Lord have called thee in righteousness, and will hold thine hand, and will keep thee, and give thee for a covenant of the people, for a light of the Gentiles; to open the blind eyes " (*Isa.* xlii. 6, 7).

" Look, ye blind, that ye may see " (*Isa.* xlii. 18).

" Bring forth the blind people that have eyes " (*Isa.* xliii. 8).

" For judgment I am come into this world, that they which see not might see " (*John* ix. 39).

" The Gentiles, unto whom now I send thee, to open their eyes" (*Acts* xxvi. 17, 18).

5. THE DARK.

The world is dark, and every man in it walketh in darkness, not knowing whither he goeth. But the light shineth in darkness,

even though the darkness comprehendeth it
not. It is to darkness such as ours that the
Light of the world has come. The light and
the love that are in him are all that the darkest soul requires. Admit that light and love,
and all is well.

"The dayspring from on high hath
visited us, to give light to them that sit
in darkness and in the shadow of death"
(*Luke* i. 78, 79).

"The people which sat in darkness saw
great light; and to them which sat in the
region and shadow of death light is sprung
up" (*Matt.* iv. 16).

"The life was the light of men. And the
light shineth in darkness . . . That was
the true Light, which lighteth every man that
cometh into the world" (*John* i. 4, 9).

"I will give thee for a light to the
Gentiles" (*Isa.* xlix. 6).

"I am the light of the world: he that
followeth me shall not walk in darkness, but
shall have the light of life" (*John* viii. 12).

"I am come a light into the world, that

whosoever believeth on me should not abide in darkness" (*John* xii. 46).

" A light to lighten the Gentiles" (*Luke* ii. 32).

"Christ shall give thee light" (*Eph.* v. 14).

"Light is come into the world" (*John* iii. 19).

" While ye have light, believe in the light, that ye may be the children of light" (*John* xii. 36).

" God, who commanded the light to shine out of darkness, hath shined in our hearts, to give the light of the knowledge of the glory of God in the face of Jesus Christ" (2 *Cor.* iv. 6).

" They looked unto him, and were lightened" (*Ps.* xxxiv. 5).

6. The Deaf.

Having ears they hear not! O awful deafness of the natural man, shutting out the music of the heavenly charmer, charm he never so wisely! Yet to the deaf God speaks;

to those who, hearing all the sounds of earth, shut their ears against the sounds of heaven. As the unstopper of the ears of the deaf, the Son of God has come!

"Bring forth the deaf that have ears" (*Isa.* xliii. 8).

"The deaf shall hear the words of the book" (*Isa.* xxix. 18).

"The ears of the deaf shall be unstopped". (*Isa.* xxxv. 5).

"Hear, ye deaf" (*Isa.* xlii. 18).

"Hear, and your soul shall live" (*Isa.* lv. 3).

"Hear, ye that are far off" (*Isa.* xxxiii. 13).

"Hear ye, and give ear; be not proud: for the Lord hath spoken" (*Jer.* xiii. 15).

"Who hath ears to hear, let him hear" (*Matt.* xiii. 9).

"He that hath an ear, let him hear what the Spirit saith unto the churches" (*Rev.* ii. 7).

7. THE SICK.

The whole head is sick, the whole heart is faint! Wounds, bruises, and putrefying sores! Disease of every form and name! Such is the sinner. "Wilt thou be made whole?" is the question which the great Healer asks; stretching out his hand and offering to heal the most diseased. Love is in his heart, and skill in his hand; what then may we not count upon? Shall we turn away from the touch of such a physician as this, or treat his words of promise as insincere or unmeaning?

" I am the Lord that healeth thee " (*Exod.* xv. 26).

" It shall come to pass, that every one that is bitten, when he looketh upon it, (the serpent of brass) shall live . . . it came to pass, that if a serpent had bitten any man, when he beheld the serpent of brass, he lived " (*Num.* xxi. 8, 9).

" Who forgiveth all thine iniquities; who healeth all thy diseases; who redeemeth thy life from destruction; who crowneth thee with loving-kindness and tender mercies " (*Ps.* ciii. 3, 4).

"He sent his word, and healed them, and delivered them from their destructions" (*Ps.* cvii. 20).

"The whole head is sick, and the whole heart faint. . . . Come now, and let us reason together, saith the Lord : though your sins be as scarlet, they shall be as white as snow" (*Isa.* i. 5, 18).

"Is there no balm in Gilead ; is there no physician there ? why then is not the health of the daughter of my people recovered ?" (*Jer.* viii. 22.)

"I will restore health unto thee, and I will heal thee of thy wounds" (*Jer.* xxx. 17).

"Behold, I will bring it health and cure, and I will cure them" (*Jer.* xxxiii. 6).

"He cast out the spirits with his word, and healed all that were sick : that it might be fulfilled which was spoken by Esaias the prophet, saying, Himself took our infirmities, and bare our sicknesses" (*Matt.* viii. 16, 17).

"They that be whole need not a physician, but they that are sick" (*Matt.* ix. 12).

" The Spirit of the Lord is upon me, because he hath anointed me to preach the gospel to the poor ; he hath sent me to heal the broken-hearted" (*Luke* iv. 18).

" The leaves of the tree were for the healing of the nations" (*Rev.* xxii. 2).

8. THE DEAD.

The dead—does God speak to *them ?* Yes. He has words for the dead in sin : and no grave is too deep, and no grave-door too firmly barricaded with rock or iron, to deny entrance to the life-giving voice. "Live" is the trumpet-sound that is going over the dead world, and the gospel of eternal life is now preached to every nation under heaven.

" He looketh upon men, and if any say, I have sinned, and perverted that which was right, and it profited me not ; he will deliver his soul from going into the pit, and his life shall see the light. Lo, all these things worketh God oftentimes with man, to bring back his soul from the pit, to be enlightened with the light of the living" (*Job* xxxiii. 27–30).

"They that dwell in the land of the shadow of death, upon them hath the light shined" (*Isa.* ix. 2).

"Thus saith the Lord God unto these bones; Behold, I will cause breath to enter into you, and ye shall live" (*Ezek.* xxxvii. 5).

"Thus saith the Lord God : Come from the four winds, O breath, and breathe upon these slain, that they may live" (*Ezek.* xxxvii. 9).

"You hath he quickened, who were dead in trespasses and sins" (*Eph.* ii. 1).

"God, who is rich in mercy, for his great love wherewith he loved us, even when we were dead in sins, hath quickened us together with Christ" (*Eph.* ii. 4, 5).

"Arise from the dead, and Christ shall give thee light" (*Eph.* v. 14).

9. THE CONDEMNED.

"Condemned already" is the Lord's description of men by nature. Law and

righteousness have pronounced against them;
they are under sentence, under wrath, under
the curse. "Condemnation" is their condition; but the Gospel comes to them with
"no condemnation" as its burden. It is to
"the condemned" that forgiveness comes;
and he who refuses to accept this character,
and to deal with God as such, must remain
unpardoned; but he who acknowledges the
condemnation and believes the Divine testimony as to pardon is a saved man.

"And the Lord passed by before him,
and proclaimed, The Lord, The Lord God,
merciful and gracious, longsuffering, and
abundant in goodness and truth, keeping
mercy for thousands, forgiving iniquity and
transgression and sin" (*Exod.* xxxiv. 6, 7).

"Thou, Lord, art good, and ready to forgive; and plenteous in mercy. . . . Thou,
O Lord, art a God full of compassion, and
gracious" (*Ps.* lxxxvi. 5, 15).

"Let the wicked forsake his way, and the
unrighteous man his thoughts: and let him
return unto the Lord, and he will have mercy
upon him; and to our God, for he will abundantly pardon" (*Isa.* lv. 7).

"I will pardon all their iniquities, whereby they have sinned, and whereby they have transgressed against me" (*Jer.* xxxiii. 8).

"Who is a God like unto thee, that pardoneth iniquity, and passeth by the transgression of the remnant of his heritage? he retaineth not his anger for ever, because he delighteth in mercy. He will turn again, he will have compassion upon us; he will subdue our iniquities; and thou wilt cast all their sins into the depths of the sea" (*Micah* vii. 18, 19).

"Be it known unto you therefore, men and brethren, that through this man is preached unto you the forgiveness of sins: and by him all that believe are justified from all things, from which ye could not be justified by the law of Moses" (*Acts* xiii. 38, 39).

"I will be merciful to their unrighteousness, and their sins and their iniquities will I remember no more" (*Heb.* viii. 12).

10. THE LOST.

It is because we are lost that we need to be saved; and the great salvation comes to us, not because we deserve it, but because we need it. Our only qualification for the Saviour is our being lost. It is only the lost that Jesus saves.

" Thou shalt call his name Jesus : for he shall save his people from their sins " (*Matt.* i. 21).

" The Son of man is come to seek and to save that which was lost" (*Luke* xix. 10).

" Whosoever shall call on the name of the Lord shall be saved " (*Acts* ii. 21).

" Neither is there salvation in any other : for there is none other name under heaven given among men, whereby we must be saved " (*Acts* iv. 12).

" If thou shalt confess with thy mouth the Lord Jesus, and shalt believe in thine heart that God hath raised him from the dead, thou shalt be saved " (*Rom.* x. 9).

" I declare unto you the gospel which I preached unto you, which also ye have received, and wherein ye stand ; by which also ye are saved, if ye keep in memory what I preached unto you " (1 *Cor.* xv. 1, 2).

" By grace are ye saved through faith"
(*Eph*. ii. 8).

" This is a faithful saying, and worthy of
all acceptation, that Christ Jesus came into
the world to save sinners" (1 *Tim*. i. 15).

" The grace of God that bringeth salvation hath appeared to all men" (*Titus* ii. 11).

" Not by works of righteousness which
we have done, but according to his mercy
he saved us" (*Titus* iii. 5).

" The Lord is not slack concerning his
promise, as some men count slackness; but is
long-suffering to us-ward, not willing that
any should perish, but that all should come
to repentance. . . . Account that the long-
suffering of our Lord is salvation" (2 *Pet*.
iii. 9, 15).

11. THE HELPLESS.

The sinner's help is in the Lord who made
heaven and earth. "God helps those who
help themselves," is man's maxim; but the
Bible truth is that God's help is for those who
have no help either in themselves or in man.

It is our helplessness that makes us so suitable for Christ and Christ for us.

"The Lord shall judge his people, and repent himself for his servants, when he seeth that their power is gone, and there is none shut up, or left" (*Deut.* xxxii. 36).

"He giveth power to the faint; and to them that have no might he increaseth strength" (*Isa.* xl. 29).

"He shall deliver the needy when he crieth; the poor also, and him that hath no helper" (*Ps.* lxxii. 12).

"They fell down, and there was none to help. Then they cried unto the Lord in their trouble, and he saved them out of their distresses" (*Ps.* cvii. 12, 13).

"When we were yet without strength, in due time Christ died for the ungodly" (*Rom.* v. 6).

12. THE POOR.

It is the poor that need riches; and for the poor God has provided the unsearchable riches. The sinner's qualification for receiving them is simply his poverty. Come to me, owning thy poverty, and I will make thee rich, is God's message in the Gospel.

" He raiseth up the poor out of the dust, and lifteth up the beggar from the dunghill " (1 *Sam.* ii. 8).

" The Spirit of the Lord is upon me, because he hath anointed me to preach the gospel to the poor " (*Luke* iv. 18).

" Ye know the grace of our Lord Jesus Christ, that, though he was rich, yet for your sakes he became poor, that ye through his poverty might be rich " (2 *Cor.* viii. 9).

" I counsel thee to buy of me gold tried in the fire, that thou mayest be rich " (*Rev.* iii. 18).

13. THE NAKED.

Without any raiment, save Adam's fig-leaves, is the sinner's state by nature. He rejects the idea of his being unclothed, or covered only with filthy rags. He is rather proud of his fig-leaves, though he admits that they require improvement. Yet it is to the naked that the raiment is presented by God; not the self-clothed or half-clothed, for God acknowledges nothing of this kind; it is to the naked that he speaks about a covering; it is to them that he holds out the Divine clothing.

"Unto Adam also and to his wife did the Lord God make coats of skins, and clothed them" (*Gen.* iii. 21).

"He hath clothed me with the garments of salvation, he hath covered me with the robe of righteousness" (*Isa.* lxi. 10).

"The father said to his servants, Bring forth the best robe, and put it on him; and put a ring on his hand, and shoes on his feet" (*Luke* xv. 22).

"Take away the filthy garments from him. Behold, I have caused thine iniquity to pass from thee, and I will clothe thee with change of raiment" (*Zech.* iii. 4).

"I spread my skirt over thee, and covered thy nakedness. Then washed I thee with water; yea, I throughly washed away thy blood from thee, and I anointed thee with oil. I clothed thee also with broidered work, and shod thee with badgers' skin, and I girded thee about with fine linen, and I covered thee with silk. I decked thee also with ornaments, and I put bracelets upon thy hands, and a chain on thy neck. And I put a jewel on thy forehead, and ear-rings in thine ears, and a beautiful crown upon thine head. Thus wast thou decked with gold and silver; and thy raiment was of fine linen, and silk, and broidered work" (*Ezek.* xvi. 8–13).

"Put ye on the Lord Jesus Christ" (*Rom.* xiii. 14).

"I counsel thee to buy of me white raiment, that thou mayest be clothed, and that the shame of thy nakedness do not appear" (*Rev.* iii. 18).

14. THE EMPTY.

He who comes to the fountain for water must come with an empty vessel; and he who comes to the fulness of Christ, must come with an empty soul — thoroughly empty — without goodness or excellence, or qualification. The full, if such there be, need not come; it is the empty that are invited. It is the sinner's emptiness that furnishes the opportunity of exhibiting and magnifying the fulness of Him who filleth all in all. He came for sinners, not for the righteous; for the feeble, not for the strong; for the unworthy, not for the worthy; for the empty, not for the full.

" Come ye, buy, and eat; yea, come, buy wine and milk without money and without price. Wherefore do ye spend money for that which is not bread? and your labour for that which satisfieth not? Hearken diligently unto me, and eat ye that which is good, and let your soul delight itself in fatness" (*Isa.* lv. 1, 2).

"Open thy mouth wide, and I will fill it. . . . Oh that my people had hearkened unto me, and Israel had walked in my ways! . . . He should have fed them also with the finest of the wheat: and with honey out of the rock should I have satisfied thee" (*Ps.* lxxxi. 10, 13, 16).

" The publican, standing afar off, would not lift up so much as his eyes unto heaven, but smote upon his breast, saying, God be merciful to me a sinner. I tell you, this man went down to his house justified rather than the other : for every one that exalteth himself shall be abased; and he that humbleth himself shall be exalted " (*Luke* xviii. 13, 14).

" When they had nothing to pay, he frankly forgave them both" (*Luke* vii. 42).

15. THE IGNORANT.

" Lack of knowledge" is one of the sorest evils which sin has wrought. " They know not me," saith the Lord. Yet no amount of ignorance can provoke God to turn away from us, or to deny us his teaching. Our dulness, our stupidity, our unteachableness, call forth his intensest compassion. For in proportion to his own vast wisdom is his appreciation of knowledge, and his desire that we should be partakers of it. In man there often is contempt for the ignorant : in God such a thing cannot be. Those possessed of a little knowledge despise those who are their inferiors in this respect. But he who is infinite in knowledge, who is the God only wise, has no such feeling. With him there is the profoundest pity to the ignorant ; pity, not merely in spite of their ignorance, but just because of it.

" Out of heaven he made thee to hear his voice, that he might instruct thee " (*Deut.* iv. 36).

" The Lord led him about, he instructed him " (*Deut.* xxxii. 10).

" Thou gavest also thy good spirit to instruct them " (*Neh.* ix. 20).

" Acquaint now thyself with him, and be at peace: thereby good shall come unto thee " (*Job* xxii. 21).

" He openeth the ears of men, and sealeth their instruction " (*Job* xxxiii. 16).

" Good and upright is the Lord : therefore will he teach sinners in the way " (*Ps.* xxv. 8).

" Come, ye children, hearken unto me : I will teach you the fear of the Lord " (*Ps.* xxxiv. 11).

" How long, ye simple ones, will ye love simplicity ? and the scorners delight in their scorning, and fools hate knowledge? Turn you at my reproof: behold, I.will pour out my spirit unto you, I will make known my words unto you" (*Prov.* i. 22).

"My son, if thou wilt receive my words, and hide my commandments with thee; so that thou incline thine ear unto wisdom, and apply thine heart to understanding; yea, if thou criest after knowledge, and liftest up thy voice for understanding; if thou seekest her as silver, and searchest for her as for hid treasures; then shalt thou understand the fear of the Lord, and find the knowledge of God. For the Lord giveth wisdom: out of his mouth cometh knowledge and understanding" (*Prov.* ii. 1–6).

"I taught them, rising up early and teaching them" (*Jer.* xxxii. 33).

"Learn of me; for I am meek and lowly in heart: and ye shall find rest unto your souls" (*Matt.* xi. 29).

"Who can have compassion on the ignorant, and on them that are out of the way" (*Heb.* v. 2).

" They shall be all taught of God"
(*John* vi. 45).

16. THE WANDERING.

" He wandereth abroad for bread, saying,
Where is it?" (Job xv. 23.) He has left his
father's house and gone into the far country.
Yes, a sinner is a houseless, homeless man,
without a roof to shelter him. " All we like
sheep have gone astray ; we have turned
every one to his own way." But the good
shepherd seeks his lost sheep ; the woman her
lost piece of silver ; the father his lost son.
The voice is heard from heaven, " Return,
return." It speaks to each wanderer of earth.

" He found him in a desert land, and in
the waste howling wilderness ; he led him
about, he instructed him, he kept him as the
apple of his eye" (*Deut*. xxxii. 10).

" The Lord alone did lead him" (*Deut*.
xxxii. 12).

" Then he is gracious unto him, and
saith, Deliver him from going down to the
pit : I have found a ransom" (*Job* xxxiii.
24).

" Lead me in thy truth, and teach me: for thou art the God of my salvation; on thee do I wait all the day " (*Ps.* xxv. 5).

" Let the wicked forsake his way, and the unrighteous man his thoughts: and let him return unto the Lord, and he will have mercy upon him " (*Isa.* lv. 7).

" To guide our feet into the way of peace" (*Luke* i. 79).

" When he was yet a great way off, his father saw him, and had compassion, and ran, and fell on his neck, and kissed him " (*Luke* xv. 20).

" To turn them from darkness to light, and from the power of Satan unto God " (*Acts* xxvi. 18).

" Who can have compassion on them that are out of the way " (*Heb.* v. 2).

17. THE UNRECONCILED.

Enemies in our minds by wicked works, is our character ere we have tasted that the Lord is gracious. But to the aliens, the strangers, the rebels, God speaks in grace. It is for the rebellious that the Son of God has received

gifts. He from whom we have alienated ourselves makes proposals of friendship to us, and
sends us the embassy of reconciliation.

"Knowing therefore the terror of the
Lord, we persuade men" (2 *Cor.* v. 11).

"Now then we are ambassadors for
Christ, as though God did beseech you by
us: we pray you in Christ's stead, be ye
reconciled to God" (2 *Cor.* v. 20).

"Fury is not in me. . . . Let him take
hold of my strength, that he may make
peace with me" (*Isa.* xxvii. 4, 5).

"When I passed by thee, and looked upon
thee, behold, thy time was the time of love;
and I spread my skirt over thee, and covered
thy nakedness: yea, I sware unto thee, and
entered into a covenant with thee, and thou
becamest mine" (*Ezek.* xvi. 8).

"Go and proclaim these words toward
the north, and say, Return, thou backsliding
Israel, saith the Lord; and I will not cause
mine anger to fall upon you: for I am merciful, saith the Lord, and I will not keep
anger for ever. Only acknowledge thine

iniquity, that thou hast transgressed against the Lord thy God, and hast scattered thy ways to the strangers under every green tree, and ye have not obeyed my voice, saith the Lord. Turn, O backsliding children, saith the Lord; for I am married unto you : and I will take you one of a city, and two of a family, and I will bring you to Zion: and I will give you pastors according to mine heart, which shall feed you with knowledge and understanding " (*Jer.* iii. 12–15).

" Say unto them, As I live, saith the Lord God, I have no pleasure in the death of the wicked; but that the wicked turn from his way and live : turn ye, turn ye from your evil ways ; for why will ye die, O house of Israel ? " (*Ezek.* xxxiii. 11.)

" I drew them with cords of a man, with bands of love " (*Hosea* xi. 4).

" Come, and let us return unto the Lord : for he hath torn, and he will heal us ; he hath smitten, and he will bind us up. After two days will he revive us : in the third day he will raise us up, and we shall live in his sight. Then shall we know, if we follow on to know the Lord: his going forth is prepared as the morning; and he shall come unto us as the rain, as the latter and former rain unto the earth. O Ephraim, what shall I do unto thee? O Judah, what shall I do unto thee? for your goodness is as a morning cloud, and as the early dew it goeth away" (*Hosea* vi. 1–4).

"How shall I give thee up, Ephraim? how shall I deliver thee, Israel? how shall I make thee as Admah? how shall I set thee as Zeboim? Mine heart is turned within me, my repentings are kindled together. I will not execute the fierceness of mine anger, I will not return to destroy Ephraim: for I am God, and not man; the Holy One in the midst of thee: and I will not enter into the city" (*Hosea* xi. 8, 9).

"Return unto the Lord thy God; for thou hast fallen by thine iniquity" (*Hosea* xiv. 1).

"Who will have all men to be saved, and to come unto the knowledge of the truth. For there is one God, and one mediator between God and men, the man Christ

Jesus; who gave himself a ransom for all, to be testified in due time" (1 *Tim.* ii. 4–6).

"If thou, Lord, shouldest mark iniquities, O Lord, who shall stand? But there is forgiveness with thee, that thou mayest be feared. I wait for the Lord, my soul doth wait, and in his word do I hope. My soul waiteth for the Lord more than they that watch for the morning: I say, more than they that watch for the morning. Let Israel hope in the Lord: for with the Lord there is mercy, and with him is plenteous redemption. And he shall redeem Israel from all his iniquities" (*Ps.* cxxx. 3–8).

"Yea, his soul draweth near unto the grave, and his life to the destroyers. If there be a messenger with him, an interpreter, one among a thousand, to show unto man his uprightness: then he is gracious unto him, and saith, Deliver him from going down to the pit: I have found a ransom. His flesh shall be fresher than a child's: he shall return to the days of his youth: he shall pray unto God, and he will be favourable unto him: and he shall see his face with joy: for he will render unto man his righteousness. He looketh upon men, and if any say, I have sinned, and perverted that which was right, and it profited me not; he will deliver his soul from going into the pit, and his life shall see the light. Lo, all these things worketh God oftentimes with man, to bring back his soul from the pit, to be enlightened with the light of the living" (*Job* xxxiii. 22–30).

"The Lord is merciful and gracious, slow to anger, and plenteous in mercy. He will not always chide; neither will he keep his anger for ever. He hath not dealt with us after our sins; nor rewarded us according to our iniquities" (*Ps.* ciii. 8–10).

"Wash you, make you clean; put away the evil of your doings from before mine eyes; cease to do evil; learn to do well; seek judgment, relieve the oppressed, judge the fatherless, plead for the widow. Come now, and let us' reason together, saith the Lord: though your sins be as scarlet, they shall be as white as snow; though they

be red like crimson, they shall be as wool"
(*Isa.* i. 16–18).

" The Lord is longsuffering to us-ward,
not willing that any should perish, but
that all should come to repentance" (2 *Pet.*
iii. 9).

" Account that the longsuffering of our
Lord is salvation" (2 *Pet.* iii. 15).

" The goodness of God leadeth thee to
repentance" (*Rom.* ii. 4).

" God hath concluded them all in unbelief,
that he might have mercy upon all" (*Rom.*
xi. 32).

" Repent ye, and be converted, that your
sins may be blotted out" (*Acts* iii. 19).

" Though thou wast angry with me,
thine anger is turned away, and thou comfortedst me" (*Isa.* xii. 1).

18. THE FAR-OFF.

They are all gone out of the way; they
have departed from God; they have gone as
far from him as they could; nay, and when he
would come nigh, they say, " Depart from us,

for we desire not the knowledge of thy ways."
Yet, in spite of their resistance and repulsion,
God has come nigh; he has sent his Son into
the far country to arrest the fugitives. They
fly, he pursues; they turn their back on him,
he turns his face to them; they reject, he
beseeches; they lose sight of him, he never
loses sight of them. The farthest-off are still
objects of his solicitude and pity.

Jesus weeping over Jerusalem is the true
expression of the mind and heart of God
toward the rebellious. Whatever distance they
have placed between God and themselves,
cannot produce any diminution of the profound compassion which he entertains toward
them in all the many windings of their perverse
flight.

"When he was yet a great way off, his
father saw him, and had compassion, and ran,
and fell on his neck, and kissed him" (*Luke*
xv. 20).

"Look unto me, and be ye saved, all the
ends of the earth" (*Isa*. xlv. 22).

"Hearken unto me, ye stouthearted, that
are far from righteousness: I bring near my
righteousness" (*Isa*. xlvi. 12, 13).

" The Lord God which gathereth the outcasts of Israel saith, Yet will I gather others to him, beside those that are gathered unto him" (*Isa.* lvi. 8).

"Seek ye me, and ye shall live" (*Amos* v. 4).

" How often would I have gathered thy children together, even as a hen gathereth her chickens under her wings, and ye would not!" (*Matt.* xxiii. 37.)

" To-day if ye will hear his voice, harden not your heart" (*Ps.* xcv. 7).

"Peace, peace to him that is far off" (*Isa.* lvii. 19).

" The promise is unto you, and to your children, and to all that are afar off" (*Acts* ii. 39).

19. THE UNWISE.

To be foolish is, in God's sight, no common evil, no trivial sin. The want of wisdom is one of the greatest of wants, so that it is said, " My people are destroyed for lack of knowledge" (Hos. iv. 6), and, "Where there is no vision, the people perish" (Prov. xxix. 18); and though that which is called " head-

knowledge," if it be alone, is insufficient, yet
the want of it is a serious evil. The God
of wisdom mourns over the foolishness of men;
he warns them of the sin of " foolishness;" he
presents his wisdom to them, that they may
be wise. Foolishness is not mere ignorance,
it is worse than this; and yet to the " simple"
and the "foolish" God speaks in grace. To
them he presents his Son, who is the wisdom
of God, that they may be " wise in Christ."

" If any of you lack wisdom, let him ask
of God, that giveth to all men liberally,
and upbraideth not; and it shall be given
him" (*James* i. 5).

" But where shall wisdom be found? and
where is the place of understanding? Man
knoweth not the price thereof; neither is it
found in the land of the living. The depth
saith, It is not in me: and the sea saith, It
is not with me. It cannot be gotten for
gold, neither shall silver be weighed for the
price thereof. It cannot be valued with the
gold of Ophir, with the precious. onyx, or
the sapphire. The gold and the crystal
cannot equal it; and the exchange of it
shall not be for jewels of fine gold. No

mention shall be made of coral, or of pearls: for the price of wisdom is above rubies. The topaz of Ethiopia shall not equal it, neither shall it be valued with pure gold. Whence then cometh wisdom? and where is the place of understanding? seeing it is hid from the eyes of all living, and kept close from the fowls of the air. Destruction and death say, We have heard the fame thereof with our ears. God understandeth the way thereof, and he knoweth the place thereof. For he looketh to the ends of the earth, and seeth under the whole heaven; to make the weight for the winds; and he weigheth the waters by measure. When he made a decree for the rain, and a way for the lightning of the thunder: then did he see it, and declare it; he prepared it, yea, and searched it out. And unto man he said, Behold, the fear of the Lord, that is wisdom; and to depart from evil is understanding " (*Job* xxviii. 12–28).

" My son, if thou wilt receive my words, and hide my commandments with thee; so that thou incline thine ear unto wisdom, and apply thine heart to understanding; yea, if thou criest after knowledge, and liftest up thy voice for understanding; if thou seekest her as silver, and searchest for her as for hid treasures; then shalt thou understand the fear of the Lord, and find the knowledge of God. For the Lord giveth wisdom: out of his mouth cometh knowledge and understanding. He layeth up sound wisdom for the righteous: he is a buckler to them that walk uprightly. He keepeth the paths of judgment, and preserveth the way of his saints. Then shalt thou understand righteousness, and judgment, and equity; yea, every good path" (*Prov.* ii. 1–9).

" Get wisdom, get understanding: forget it not; neither decline from the words of my mouth. Forsake her not, and she shall preserve thee: love her, and she shall keep thee. Wisdom is the principal thing; therefore get wisdom: and with all thy getting get understanding" (*Prov.* iv. 5–7).

" The testimony of the Lord is sure, making wise the simple" (*Ps.* xix. 7).

" Bow down thine ear, and hear the words of the wise" (*Prov.* xxii. 17).

" Doth not wisdom cry? and understanding put forth her voice? She standeth in the top of high places, by the way in the places of the paths. She crieth at the gates, at the entry of the city, at the coming in at the doors. Unto you, O men, I call; and my voice is to the sons of man. O ye simple, understand wisdom: and, ye fools, be ye of an understanding heart" (*Prov.* viii. 1–5).

" Now therefore hearken unto me, O ye children: for blessed are they that keep my ways. Hear instruction, and be wise, and refuse it not. Blessed is the man that heareth me, watching daily at my gates, waiting at the posts of my doors. For whoso findeth me findeth life, and shall obtain favour of the Lord" (*Prov.* viii. 32–35).

" Wisdom hath builded her house, she hath hewn out her seven pillars; she hath killed her beasts; she hath mingled her wine; she hath also furnished her table.

She hath sent forth her maidens: she crieth upon the highest places of the city, Whoso is simple, let him turn in hither: as for him that wanteth understanding, she saith to him, Come, eat of my bread, and drink of the wine which I have mingled. Forsake the foolish, and live; and go in the way of understanding" (*Prov.* ix. 1-6).

20. THE REBELLIOUS.

The sons of Adam have rebelled against the Lord. He has nourished and brought them up as children; but they have rebelled against him. They are a rebellious generation, with a revolting and rebellious heart. Yet to such the message of reconciliation comes. Be no more rebellious. Enter into friendship with me; take hold of my strength and make peace with me, and ye shall make peace with me (Isa. xxvii. 5). No amount of resistance and alienation can alter the tender mercy of our God, or make his promises of grace less true and real.

" Thou hast received gifts for men; yea, for the rebellious also, that the Lord God might dwell among them " (*Ps.* lxviii. 18).

" I am sought of them that asked not for
me; I am found of them that sought me
not: I said, Behold me, behold me, unto a
nation that was not called by my name. I
have spread out my hands all the day unto
a rebellious people, which walketh in a way
that was not good, after their own thoughts "
(*Isa.* lxv. 1, 2).

" Wherefore remember, that ye being in
time past Gentiles in the flesh, who are
called Uncircumcision by that which is
called the Circumcision in the flesh made by
hands; that at that time ye were without
Christ, being aliens from the commonwealth
of Israel, and strangers from the covenants
of promise, having no hope, and without
God in the world: but now in Christ
Jesus ye who sometimes were far off are
made nigh by the blood of Christ. For he
is our peace, who hath made both one, and
hath broken down the middle wall of par-
tition between us; having abolished in his
flesh the enmity, even the law of commandments contained in ordinances; for to make
in himself of twain one new man, so making

peace; and that he might reconcile both unto God in one body by the cross, having slain the enmity thereby: and came and preached peace to you which were afar off, and to them that were nigh. For through him we both have access by one Spirit unto the Father. Now therefore ye are no more strangers and foreigners, but fellow-citizens with the saints, and of the household of God" (*Eph.* ii. 11–19).

———◆———

Thus to all kinds and classes of men God speaks in his grace; so that there is no one upon this earth that can say, There is no message for me. He overlooks none; nor shall there be any hereafter among the lost who shall be able to cast blame upon God, and say, I perished because there was no grace and no promise for me.

All the promises meet in Jesus. They are his words of grace. He speaks in them to the sons of men. They are his messages, his invitations; they obtain all their power, their light, their suitableness from him. Apart from him they are nothing; in connection with him they sparkle with all the brightness of love.

The cross of Christ is the one centre to which they point us; for only through that cross can any one promise become possible of fulfilment. There the person and work of the Substitute are fully unfolded; the great propitiation makes each promise not only a possibility but a reality—a righteous reality; and the deep river of God's free love gushes out in strength from the foot of the wondrous tree, dividing itself not merely into four, but into a thousand channels—each promise a separate channel or stream, filled to the brim with living water.

CHAPTER II.

FOR THE SAINT.

THE Romish Church has so long perverted this name, and spread the false use of it so widely, that the original signification of the word has been lost sight of. Certainly it ought to be restored. God's designation for his people must be the best.

In nearly all the Epistles, the word "saint" occurs as the common name for Christians. "Brethren," "called ones" (Rom. i. 7), "the sanctified in Christ Jesus" (1 Cor. i. 2), "beloved of God" (Rom. i. 7), "elect" (1 Pet. i. 2), "the faithful" (Eph. i. 1), "sons of God" (1 John iii. 1), are designations frequently found; but the most usual is "saints," as when Paul writes "to the *saints* which are in Ephesus," "to the *saints* in Christ Jesus which are at Philippi," "to the *saints* and faithful brethren in Christ which are at Colosse."

A saint, then, is one set apart for God by the sprinkling of the blood of Christ upon him, through faith in the name of Jesus. It is not used in Scripture to signify an "advanced Christian," or a "peculiarly holy" man; but simply one who has accepted God's testimony regarding the blood of his Son. It is a name not merely applicable to spiritual *character*, but to *condition*, or standing, in the sight of God. Having received the Divine record or good news concerning the great propitiation, we are transferred from the ranks of the "unclean" to the "clean;" we are washed, we are sanctified, we are justified, in the name of the Lord Jesus, and by the Spirit of our God (1 Cor. vi. 11). We become "saints," not indeed according to the Romish use of the name, but according to that of the Apostles and the early Church.

Being thus personally accepted of God, through the belief of the truth, we receive the indwelling Spirit, and the inward process of purifying begins. And with the purifying begins the discipline; for our whole life is one continuous training, one unceasing process of learning. We are placed in Christ's school, with the Holy Spirit for our teacher. Nor is it training or education merely which we undergo; we are called on to do, to fight, to suffer, to run, to watch, to serve, to "withstand," and to "stand."

To these varied states or duties or trials the promises are addressed.

1. OF PEACE.

It is the gospel of peace that is preached, and on our reception of it we enter into peace. Christ is our peace; he has made peace through the blood of his cross. And this peace stands firm. It is stable and immortal; able to bear the buffetings of this world's vicissitudes, of the fightings without and the fears within. Our God is the God of peace; our path is the path of peace; and our inheritance is the heritage of peace. The good news to us from heaven are all of peace, peace with God, peace in God, the peace of God —peace like a river, peace that passeth all understanding—peace derived not from aught in or about ourselves, but wholly from what God has revealed to us concerning the person and the cross of his Son.

" Being justified by faith, we have peace with God through our Lord Jesus Christ " (*Rom.* v. 1).

" Peace I leave with you, my peace I give unto you: not as the world giveth, give I unto you " (*John* xiv. 27).

" Let the peace of God rule in your hearts, to the which also ye are called in one body " (*Col.* iii. 15).

" Now the Lord of peace himself give you peace always by all means " (2 *Thess.* iii. 16).

" Peace be to the brethren, and love with faith, from God the Father and the Lord Jesus Christ " (*Eph.* vi. 23).

" Peace be with you all that are in Christ Jesus " (1 *Pet.* v. 14).

" The fruit of the Spirit is love, joy, peace " (*Gal.* v. 22).

" Peace to every man that worketh good " (*Rom.* ii. 10).

" The God of hope fill you with all joy and peace in believing " (*Rom.* xv. 13).

" Peace be on them, and mercy, and upon the Israel of God " (*Gal.* vi. 16).

" Your feet shod with the preparation of the gospel of peace " (*Eph.* vi. 15).

" Grace be unto you, and peace, from God our Father and the Lord Jesus Christ " (*Col.* i. 2).

" These things I have spoken unto you, that in me ye might have peace. In the world ye shall have tribulation: but be of good cheer; I have overcome the world" (*John* xvi. 33).

" The peace of God, which passeth all understanding, shall keep your hearts and minds through Christ Jesus" (*Phil.* iv. 7).

" His soul shall dwell at ease" (*Ps.* xxv. 13).

" The Lord will bless his people with peace" (*Ps.* xxix. 11).

" He will speak peace unto his people and to his saints" (*Ps.* lxxxv. 8).

" Great peace have they which love thy law: and nothing shall offend them" (*Ps.* cxix. 165).

" Her ways are ways of pleasantness, and all her paths are peace" (*Prov.* iii. 17).

" Thou wilt keep him in perfect peace, whose mind is stayed on thee" (*Isa.* xxvi. 3).

" Let him take hold of my strength, that he may make peace with me; and he shall make peace with me" (*Isa.* xxvii. 5).

" The work of righteousness shall be peace; and the effect of righteousness quietness and assurance for ever" (*Isa.* xxxii. 17).

" The God of peace shall be with you " (*Phil.* iv. 9).

2. OF JOY.

Our joy begins in the belief of the glad tidings. The three thousand at Jerusalem rejoiced; the jailer rejoiced. A believed gospel fills the soul with gladness. We joy not in ourselves, but in God, through our Lord Jesus Christ. The more we drink into the Gospel the more does this gladness increase. The believing man is brought into a region of joy, and into contact with truths and objects which daily increase his joy. A believed gospel makes a happy man. God wishes us to be joyful, to joy in God, to be partakers of his joy.

" Let the righteous be glad; let them rejoice before God: yea, let them exceedingly rejoice" (*Ps.* lxviii. 3).

" These things have I spoken unto you,

that my joy might remain in you, and that your joy might be full" (*John* xv. 11).

"Finally, my brethren, rejoice in the Lord. . . . Rejoice in the Lord alway: and again I say, Rejoice" (*Phil.* iii. 1; iv. 4).

"Thou shalt have thy delight in the Almighty, and shalt lift up thy face unto God" (*Job* xxii. 26).

"The righteous shall be glad in the Lord" (*Ps.* lxiv. 10).

"In thy name shall they rejoice all the day" (*Ps.* lxxxix. 16).

"Her saints shall shout aloud for joy" (*Ps.* cxxxii. 16).

"Your heart shall rejoice, and your bones shall flourish like an herb" (*Isa.* lxvi. 14).

"Our heart shall rejoice in him, because we have trusted in his holy name" (*Ps.* xxxiii. 21).

"In the shadow of thy wings will I rejoice" (*Ps.* lxiii. 7).

"I will rejoice in the Lord, I will joy in the God of my salvation" (*Hab.* iii. 18).

" The joy of the Lord is your strength "
(*Neh.* viii. 10).

" In thy presence is fulness of joy ; 'at thy
right hand there are pleasures for evermore "
(*Ps.* xvi. 11).

" Joy cometh in the morning " (*Ps.*
xxx. 5).

" They that sow in tears shall reap in
joy " (*Ps.* cxxvi. 5).

" God giveth to a man that is good in
his sight wisdom, and knowledge, and joy "
(*Eccles.* ii. 26).

" Go thy way, eat thy bread with joy,
and drink thy wine with a merry heart "
(*Eccles.* ix. 7).

" With joy shall ye draw water out of
the wells of salvation " (*Isa.* xii. 3).

" The meek shall increase their joy in the
Lord, and the poor among men shall rejoice
in the Holy One of Israel " (*Isa.* xxix. 19).

" Ask, and ye shall receive, that your joy
may be full " (*John* xvi. 24).

" These things I speak in the world, that

they might have my joy fulfilled in themselves" (*John* xvii. 13).

"The disciples were filled with joy, and
with the Holy Ghost" (*Acts* xiii. 52).

"The God of hope fill you with all joy
and peace in believing, that ye may abound
in hope, through the power of the Holy
Ghost" (*Rom.* xv. 13).

"We are helpers of your joy" (2 *Cor.*
i. 24).

"The fruit of the Spirit is love, joy,
peace" (*Gal.* v. 22).

"I know that I shall abide and continue
with you all for your furtherance and joy of
faith" (*Phil.* i. 25).

"Having received the word in much
affliction, with joy of the Holy Ghost"
(1 *Thess.* i. 6).

"Believing, ye rejoice with joy unspeakable and full of glory" (1 *Pet.* i. 8).

"Rejoice, inasmuch as ye are partakers of
Christ's sufferings; that, when his glory shall
be revealed, ye may be glad also with exceeding joy" (1 *Pet.* iv. 13).

" These things write we unto you, that your joy may be full " (1 *John* i. 4).

" To present you faultless before the presence of his glory with exceeding joy " (*Jude* 24).

" We also joy in God through our Lord Jesus Christ" (*Rom.* v. 11).

" For the same cause also do ye joy, and rejoice with me " (*Phil.* ii. 18).

" Let them that love thy name be joyful in thee " (*Ps.* v. 11).

" Blessed is the people that know the joyful sound " (*Ps.* lxxxix. 15).

" Let the children of Zion be joyful in their King " (*Ps.* cxlix. 2).

" I will make them joyful in my house of prayer " (*Isa.* lvi. 7).

" They shall obtain joy and gladness " (*Isa.* xxxv. 10).

" Ye shall have a song, . . . and gladness of heart " (*Isa.* xxx. 29).

" Serve the Lord with gladness " (*Ps.* c. 2).

"Gladness is sown for the upright in heart" (*Ps.* xcvii. 11).

"Thou hast girded me with gladness" (*Ps.* xxx. 11).

"Thou hast put gladness in my heart" (*Ps.* iv. 7).

"I will be glad and rejoice in thy mercy" (*Ps.* xxxi. 7).

"Be glad in the Lord, and rejoice, ye righteous" (*Ps.* xxxii. 11).

"Be glad and rejoice, and give honour to him : for the marriage of the Lamb is come" (*Rev.* xix. 7).

3. OF COMFORT.

"Everlasting consolation" is our heritage ; not comfort for a day, but for a lifetime ; nay, for ever.   God's desire in behalf of his own is that they should be comforted.   Though in heaviness through manifold temptations, they are yet supplied and sustained with Divine consolation, which never fails.   It is "consolation in Christ," and there is no sorrow upon earth which will not yield to this.   The things seen and temporal contain much to disquiet; but the things unseen and eternal are full of comfort and rest. The less we dwell upon the former, and the more we meditate on the latter, the more will our consolation abound.

"Comfort ye, comfort ye my people, saith your God" (*Isa.* xl. 1).

"Fear thou not; for I am with thee: be not dismayed; for I am thy God: I will strengthen thee; yea, I will help thee; yea, I will uphold thee with the right hand of my righteousness" (*Isa.* xli. 10).

"A bruised reed shall he not break, and the smoking flax shall he not quench" (*Isa.* xlii. 3).

"Who is among you that feareth the Lord, that obeyeth the voice of his servant, that walketh in darkness, and hath no light? let him trust in the name of the Lord, and stay upon his God" (*Isa.* l. 10).

"I, even I, am he that comforteth you: who art thou, that thou shouldest be afraid of a man that shall die, and of the son of man which shall be made as grass; and forgettest the Lord thy Maker, that hath stretched forth the heavens, and laid the foundations of the earth ; and hast feared continually every day because of the fury of the oppressor, as if he were ready to destroy And where is the fury of the oppressor ? (*Isa.* li. 12, 13.)

" Thou hast enlarged me when I was in distress " (*Ps.* iv. 1).

" Thou art with me ; thy rod and thy staff they comfort me " (*Ps.* xxiii. 4).

" Though I walk in the midst of trouble, thou wilt revive me " (*Ps.* cxxxviii. 7).

" The Lord will not suffer the soul of the righteous to famish " (*Prov.* x. 3).

" When thou passest through the waters, I will be with thee ; and through the rivers, they shall not overflow thee : when thou walkest through the fire, thou shalt not be burned ; neither shall the flame kindle upon thee " (*Isa.* xliii. 2).

" Thou, which hast showed me great and sore troubles, shalt quicken me again, and shalt bring me up again from the depths of the earth. Thou shalt increase my greatness, and comfort me on every side" (*Ps.* lxxi. 20, 21).

"He healeth the broken in heart, and bindeth up their wounds" (*Ps.* cxlvii. 3).

"Though thou wast angry with me, thine anger is turned away, and thou comfortedst me" (*Isa.* xii. 1).

"The Spirit of the Lord God is upon me; because the Lord hath anointed me to bind up the broken-hearted . . . to comfort all that mourn; to appoint unto them that mourn in Zion, to give unto them beauty for ashes, the oil of joy for mourning, the garment of praise for the spirit of heaviness" (*Isa.* lxi. 1–3).

4. OF BLESSEDNESS.

Our blessedness has its fountain-head above. But the streams have found their way down to earth, and flow all through the "camp of the saints." God means that his saints should be blessed men; partakers of that which makes him "the blessed God;" drinking of the rivers of pleasure that are with him.

" Blessed is the people that know the joyful
sound ; " and the more we know of this joyful
sound, the more shall we be filled with the
blessedness which it contains.

" Happy art thou, O Israel : who is like
unto thee, O people saved by the Lord "
(*Deut.* xxxiii. 29).

" Behold, happy is the man whom God
correcteth " (*Job* v. 17).

" Blessed is the man that walketh not in
the counsel of the ungodly " (*Ps.* i. 1).

" Blessed is he whose transgression is forgiven, whose sin is covered.   Blessed is the
man unto whom the Lord imputeth not
iniquity, and in whose spirit there is no
guile " (*Ps.* xxxii. 1, 2).

" O taste and see that the Lord is good :
blessed is the man that trusteth in him "
(*Ps.* xxxiv. 8).

" Blessed are the undefiled in the way,
who walk in the law of the Lord.   Blessed
are they that keep his testimonies, and that
seek him with the whole heart " (*Ps.* cxix.
1. 2).

" Happy is the man that findeth wisdom, and the man that getteth understanding " (*Prov.* iii. 13).

" Blessed is the man that heareth me, watching daily at my gates, waiting at the posts of my doors " (*Prov.* viii. 34).

" Blessed are they that do his commandments, that they may have right to the tree of life, and may enter in through the gates into the city " (*Rev.* xxii. 14).

" Blessed are they whose iniquities are forgiven, and whose sins are covered. Blessed is the man to whom the Lord will not impute sin " (*Rom.* iv. 7, 8).

" Blessed are they that dwell in thy house : they will be still praising thee. Blessed is the man whose strength is in thee ; in whose heart are the ways " (*Ps.* lxxxiv. 4).

" Come, ye blessed of my Father, inherit the kingdom prepared for you from the foundation of the world " (*Matt.* xxv. 34).

" Blessed and holy is he that hath part in the first resurrection " (*Rev.* xx. 6).

"Blessed be the God and Father of our Lord Jesus Christ, who hath blest us with all spiritual blessings in heavenly places in Christ" (*Eph.* i. 3).

"Knowing that ye are thereunto called, that ye should inherit a blessing" (1 *Pet.* iii. 9).

"Blessed are they that keep my ways" (*Prov.* viii. 32).

"Ye are blessed of the Lord which made heaven and earth" (*Ps.* cxv. 15).

"This man shall be blessed in his deed" (*James* i. 25).

"Blessed are they which are called unto the marriage supper of the Lamb" (*Rev.* xix. 9).

5. ENCOURAGEMENT.

Let nothing cast down a saint. Great is the battle and glorious is the victory of faith. If God be for us, who can be against us? Let us be without carefulness. Let us be of good cheer; resolute and undaunted in every good word and work.

" Hearken unto me, ye that know righteousness, the people in whose heart is my law ; fear ye not the reproach of men, neither be ye afraid of their revilings. For the moth shall eat them up like a garment, and the worm shall eat them like wool : but my righteousness shall be for ever, and my salvation from generation to generation " (*Isa.* li. 7, 8).

" Be of good cheer ; I have overcome the world " (*John* xvi. 33).

" Let not your heart be troubled : ye believe in God, believe also in me. In my Father's house are many mansions. I go to prepare a place for you. And if I go and prepare a place for you, I will come again, and receive you to myself ; that where I am, there ye may be also " (*John* xiv. 1–3).

" Be careful for nothing ; but in everything by prayer and supplication with thanksgiving let your requests be made known unto God " (*Phil.* iv. 6).

" Say to them that are of a fearful heart, Be strong, fear not : behold, your God will come with vengeance, even God with a recompence; he will come and save you" (*Isa.* xxxv. 4).

"There shall not any man be able to stand before thee all the days of thy life: as I was with Moses, so I will be with thee: I will not fail thee nor forsake thee. Be strong and of a good courage. . . . Be thou strong and very courageous. . . . Be strong and of a good courage; be not afraid, neither be thou dismayed: for the Lord thy God is with thee whithersoever thou goest" (*Josh.* i. 5–9).

"Be of good cheer; it is I; be not afraid" (*Matt.* xiv. 27).

"Be strong and of good courage, and do it: fear not, nor be dismayed: for the Lord God, even my God, will be with thee; he will not fail thee, nor forsake thee" (1 *Chron.* xxviii. 20).

"Watch ye, stand fast in the faith, quit you like men, be strong" (1 *Cor.* xvi. 13).

"O man greatly beloved, fear not: peace be unto thee, be strong, yea, be strong" (*Dan.* x. 19).

"David encouraged himself in the Lord his God" (1 *Sam.* xxx. 6).

"Deal courageously, and the Lord shall be with the good" (2 *Chron.* xix. 11).

6. OF UPHOLDING.

No Christian knows how much he needs to be held up till he has stumbled or fallen. At first he thinks that, having been set upon his feet, he can keep himself steadfast, that, having been placed upon a rock, he is secure. There is, however, the holding up as well as the lifting up; and for this we require to be every moment indebted to the free love of God and to his mighty power. Yesterday's upholding will not do for to-day, nor to-day's for to-morrow. It must be fresh and new; as constant as the air; as regular as the sap which is every moment ascending the tree and doing in every part thereof its vitalizing work. For thus it is that we live by faith upon the Son of God.

"Thou hast holden me by my right hand" (*Ps.* lxxiii. 23).

"He will keep the feet of his saints, and the wicked shall be silent in darkness; for by strength shall no man prevail" (1 *Sam.* ii. 9).

"He will not suffer thy foot to be moved: he that keepeth thee will not slumber" (*Ps.* cxxi. 3).

"The Lord upholdeth him with his hand" (*Ps.* xxxvii. 24).

"The Lord upholdeth the righteous" (*Ps.* xxxvii. 17).

"The Lord upholdeth all that fall (are falling), and raiseth up all those that be bowed down" (*Ps.* cxlv. 14).

"Thy right hand upholdeth me" (*Ps.* lxiii. 8).

"Fear thou not; for I am with thee: be not dismayed; for I am thy God: I will strengthen thee; yea, I will help thee; yea, I will uphold thee with the right hand of my righteousness" (*Isa.* xli. 10).

"Uphold me with thy free Spirit" (*Ps.* li. 12).

"I pray not that thou shouldest take them out of the world, but that thou shouldest keep them from the evil" (*John* xvii. 15).

"Who shall also confirm you unto the end, that ye may be blameless in the day of our Lord Jesus Christ" (1 *Cor.* i. 8).

"Holy Father, keep through thine own name those whom thou hast given me" (*John* xvii. 11).

"Who shall stablish you, and keep you from evil" (2 *Thess.* iii. 3). '

"Kept by the power of God through faith unto salvation" (1 *Pet.* i. 5).

"Preserved in Jesus Christ" (*Jude* 1).

"To him that is of power to stablish you according to my gospel: to God only wise, be glory through Jesus Christ for ever" (*Rom.* xvi. 25, 27).

"Unto him that is able to keep you from falling, and to present you faultless before the presence of his glory with exceeding joy, to the only wise God our Saviour, be glory and majesty, dominion and power, both now and ever. Amen" (*Jude* 24).

7. OF DELIVERANCE.

Our first deliverance is from the burden of our iniquities. We believe, and are delivered. We believe, and the chains are broken. But *one* deliverance is not all we need. The life of a saint is a constant series of deliverances, greater or less; temporal or spiritual. Enemy after enemy, like wave upon wave, comes against him, and he has no might to resist or overcome. Each day seems to shut him up in some new way; but each day he is liberated. Each day the fiery darts are aimed at him; but his shield quenches them. His life is all one long deliverance, through the love and power of Him who delivered him at first.

"Call upon me in the day of trouble: I will deliver thee, and thou shalt glorify me" (*Ps.* l. 15).

"He shall deliver the needy when he crieth; the poor also, and him that hath no helper" (*Ps.* lxxii. 12).

"The Lord will deliver him in time of trouble" (*Ps.* xli. 1).

" Because he hath set his love upon me,
therefore will I deliver him" (*Ps.* xci. 14).

" Our God whom we serve is able to
deliver us, and he will deliver us" (*Dan.*
iii. 17).

" The righteous is delivered out of
trouble. Through knowledge shall the just
be delivered. The seed of the righteous shall
be delivered" (*Prov.* xi. 8, 9, 21).

" The Lord knoweth how to deliver the
godly out of temptations" (2 *Pet.* ii. 9).

" Who delivered us from so great a
death, and doth deliver: in whom we trust
that he will yet deliver us" (2 *Cor.* i. 10).

" I have made, and I will bear; even I
will carry, and will deliver" (*Isa.* xlvi. 4).

" Whoso walketh wisely, he shall be
delivered" (*Prov.* xxviii. 26).

" Whosoever shall call on the name of
the Lord shall be delivered" (*Joel* ii. 32).

" He delivereth and rescueth, and he
worketh signs and wonders in heaven and in
earth" (*Dan.* vi. 27).

"The Lord thy God walketh in the midst of thy camp, to deliver thee, and to give up thine enemies before thee" (*Deut.* xxiii. 14).

"The eternal God is thy refuge, and underneath are the everlasting arms: and he shall thrust out the enemy from before thee; and shall say, Destroy them" (*Deut.* xxxiii. 27).

"He preserveth the souls of his saints: he delivereth them out of the hand of the wicked" (*Ps.* xcvii. 10).

"In the floods of great waters they shall not come nigh unto him" (*Ps.* xxxii. 6).

"He redeemeth thy life from destruction" (*Ps.* ciii. 4).

"Because thou hast kept the word of my patience, I also will keep thee from the hour of temptation, which shall come upon all the world, to try them that dwell upon the earth" (*Rev.* iii. 10).

8. OF STRENGTH.

Out of weakness we are made strong; and our strength is all the more sufficient and the more blessed because it is not our own, but is that of another, even of Him who died for us and who rose again, who was crucified through weakness, but who liveth by the power of God. The might of the mighty One thus becomes as truly ours as if it were really our own; for it is as free, as near, as much at our disposal, as if it were within us, and not without us. The fact of the fountain-head being in heaven does not make our hourly supply at all more difficult, or precarious, or uncertain, than if a separate source existed within each of us. Faith takes, every moment, all that is needed, as easily and as quickly as if the fountain were within, not without. For to faith, place and distance are really nothing, just as to the God on whom faith leans, place and distance are nothing.

" Will he plead against me with his great power? No; but he would put strength in me" (*Job* xxiii. 6).

" The Lord is their strength in the time of trouble. And the Lord shall help them and deliver them" (*Ps.* xxxvii. 39, 40).

"Strengthen ye the weak hands, and confirm the feeble knees" (*Isa.* xxxv. 3).

" He that hath clean hands shall be stronger and stronger " (*Job* xvii. 9).

" Be strong in the grace that is in Christ Jesus " (2 *Tim.* ii. 1).

" Be strong in the Lord, and in the power of his might " (*Eph.* vi. 10).

" Stand fast in the faith, quit you like men, be strong " (1 *Cor.* xvi. 13).

" Fear not, but let your hands be strong " (*Zech.* viii. 13).

" The people that do know their God shall be strong, and do exploits " (*Dan.* xi. 32).

" Say to them that are of a fearful heart, Be strong " (*Isa.* xxxv. 4).

" Ye are strong, and the word of God abideth in you " (1 *John* ii. 14).

" When I am weak, then am I strong " (2 *Cor.* xii. 10).

" Let the weak say, I am strong " (*Joel* iii. 10).

" I can do all things through Christ which strengtheneth me " (*Phil.* iv. 13).

" I will strengthen them in the Lord"
(*Zech.* x. 12).

"Wait on the Lord, be of good courage,
and he shall strengthen thine heart" (*Ps.*
xxvii. 14).

" Strengthened with all might, according
to his glorious power" (*Col.* i. 11).

9. OF PROTECTION.

God saves and shields. He is the "shield"
and "horn" of our salvation. Not only does
he defend us, but he himself is our defence.
Not only does he ward off blows, but he himself is our shield and buckler. O excellent
defence! Better than the munition of rocks;
more secure than that of tower or fortress!
"There shall no evil happen to the just." He is
safe beneath the feathers of the almighty wing.

" The Lord also will be a refuge for the
oppressed, a refuge in times of trouble" (*Ps.*
ix. 9).

" In the time of trouble he shall hide
me in his pavilion: in the secret of his
tabernacle shall he hide me; he shall set me
up upon a rock" (*Ps.* xxvii. 5).

" The Lord is good, a strong hold in the day of trouble; and he knoweth them that trust in him" (*Nahum* i. 7).

" He that dwelleth in the secret place of the most High shall abide under the shadow of the Almighty. I will say of the Lord, He is my refuge and my fortress: my God; in him will I trust. He shall cover thee with his feathers, and under his wings shalt thou trust: his truth shall be thy shield and buckler" (*Ps.* xci. 1, 2, 4).

" When thou passest through the waters, I will be with thee; and through the rivers, they shall not overflow thee: when thou walkest through the fire, thou shalt not be burned; neither shall the flame kindle upon thee" (*Isa.* xliii. 2).

" Be not afraid of sudden fear, neither of the desolation of the wicked, when it cometh. For the Lord shall be thy confidence, and shall keep thy foot from being taken" (*Prov.* iii. 25, 26).

" The angel of the Lord encampeth round about them that fear him, and delivereth them" (*Ps.* xxxiv. 7).

"He shall give his angels charge over thee, to keep thee in all thy ways" (*Ps.* xci 11).

"Thou art my hiding-place; thou shalt preserve me from trouble" (*Ps.* xxxii. 7).

"Thou, Lord, wilt bless the righteous; with favour wilt thou compass him as with a shield" (*Ps.* v. 12).

"My soul, wait thou only upon God; for my expectation is from him. He only is my rock and my salvation: he is my defence; I shall not be moved. In God is my salvation and my glory: the rock of my strength, and my refuge, is in God. Trust in him at all times; ye people, pour out your heart before him: God is a refuge for us" (*Ps.* lxii. 5–8).

"The name of the Lord is a strong tower: the righteous runneth into it, and is safe" (*Prov.* xviii. 10).

"Behold, God is my salvation; I will trust, and not be afraid: for the Lord Jehovah is my strength and my song; he also is become my salvation" (*Isa.* xii. 2).

"Trust ye in the Lord for ever: for in the Lord Jehovah is everlasting strength" (*Isa.* xxvi. 4).

10. OF WISDOM.

Christ is our *wisdom;* we are wise in Christ, for in him are hid all the treasures of wisdom and knowledge; he, "of God, is made unto us wisdom." So that in having him we have wisdom; and we have *him,* simply in receiving the Father's testimony to him. As he that hath the Son hath *life,* so he that hath the Son hath *wisdom.* All wisdom separate from Him who is "the wisdom of God" and "the Word of God" is vain. All the wisdom spoken or in Scripture from beginning to end is in connection with him. He is the Alpha and the Omega of all knowledge, the soul of all truth. "The testimony of Jesus is" not only "the spirit of prophecy," but of all Scripture together.

"If any of you lack wisdom, let him ask of God, that giveth to all men liberally, and upbraideth not; and it shall be given him" (*James* i. 5).

" In the hidden part thou shalt make me to know wisdom " (*Ps.* li. 6).

" To one is given, by the Spirit, the word of wisdom " (1 *Cor.* xii. 8).

" Happy is the man that findeth wisdom, and the man that getteth understanding " (*Prov.* iii. 13).

" They that seek the Lord understand all things " (*Prov.* xxviii. 5).

" Then shall we know, if we follow on to know the Lord " (*Hosea* vi. 3).

" We know that the Son of God is come, and hath given us an understanding, that we may know him that is true " (1 *John* v. 20).

" Lo, I have given thee a wise and an understanding heart " (1 *Kings* iii. 12).

" O God, thou hast taught me from my youth " (*Ps.* lxxi. 17).

" The Lord giveth wisdom : out of his mouth cometh knowledge and understanding. He layeth up sound wisdom for the righteous " (*Prov.* ii. 6, 7).

" God giveth to a man that is good in

his sight wisdom, and knowledge, and joy "
(*Eccles.* ii. 26).

" I will give them an heart to know me,
that I am the Lord " (*Jer.* xxiv. 7).

" All thy children shall be taught of the
Lord " (*Isa.* liv. 13).

" Thou gavest thy good spirit to instruct
them " (*Neh.* ix. 20).

" When he, the Spirit of truth, is come,
he will guide you into all truth " (*John*
xvi. 13).

" Ye have an unction from the Holy One,
and ye know all things " (1 *John* ii. 20).

" We do not cease to pray for you, and
to desire that ye might be filled with the
knowledge of his will in all wisdom and
spiritual understanding " (*Col.* i. 9).

" I pray, that your love may abound
yet more and more in knowledge and in all
judgment " (*Phil.* i. 9).

" That ye may be able to comprehend,
with all saints, what is the breadth, and
length, and depth, and height; and to know
the love of Christ, which passeth knowledge,

that ye might be filled with all the fulness
of God" (*Eph.* iii. 18, 19).

"That the God of our Lord Jesus Christ,
the Father of glory, may give unto you the
spirit of wisdom and revelation in the knowledge of him: the eyes of your understanding
being enlightened; that ye may know what
is the hope of his calling, and what the
riches of the glory of his inheritance in the
saints" (*Eph.* i. 17, 18).

"As it is written, Eye hath not seen, nor
ear heard, neither have entered into the heart
of man, the things which God hath prepared
for them that love him. But God hath
revealed them unto us by his Spirit: for the
Spirit searcheth all things, yea, the deep
things of God. For what man knoweth the
things of a man, save the spirit of man
which is in him? even so the things of God
knoweth no man, but the Spirit of God.
Now we have received, not the spirit of the
world, but the spirit which is of God; that
we might know the things that are freely
given to us of God" (1 *Cor.* ii. 9–12).

"The Holy Ghost, whom the Father will

send in my name, he shall teach you all things" (*John* xiv. 26).

"I will pour out my spirit unto you, I will make known my words unto you" (*Prov.* i. 23).

"They shall be all taught of God" (*John* vi. 45).

"It is given unto you to know the mysteries of the kingdom of heaven" (*Matt.* xiii. 11).

"He giveth wisdom unto the wise, and knowledge to them that know understanding: he revealeth the deep and secret things" (*Dan.* ii. 21, 22).

"We have also a more sure word of prophecy, whereunto ye do well that ye take heed, as unto a light that shineth in a dark place" (2 *Pet.* i. 19).

"I am the Lord thy God, which teacheth thee to profit, which leadeth thee by the way that thou shouldest go" (*Isa.* xlviii. 17).

"Then opened he their understanding that they might understand the scriptures" (*Luke* xxiv. 45).

11. OF GUIDANCE.

Our way winds, and the road is rough, and the world is dark, and enemies are many, and snares are subtilely laid for our feet. We need a guide, and that guide must be Divine. Jehovah is to us now what he was to Israel when he led them through the wilderness with his pillar-cloud.

" He will be our guide even unto death" (*Ps.* xlviii. 14).

" The meek will he guide in judgment, and the meek will he teach his way" (*Ps.* xxv. 9).

" I will guide thee with mine eye" (*Ps.* xxxii. 8).

" The Lord shall guide thee continually" (*Isa.* lviii. 11).

" He guided them in the wilderness like a flock" (*Ps.* lxxviii. 52).

" O send out thy light and thy truth : let them lead me" (*Ps.* xliii. 3).

" I lead in the way of righteousness ; in

the midst of the paths of judgment" (*Prov.* viii. 20).

"I will lead them in paths that they have not known" (*Isa.* xlii. 16).

"He leadeth me beside the still waters" (*Ps.* xxiii. 2).

"I am the Lord thy God which leadeth thee" (*Isa.* xlviii. 17).

"He led them forth by the right way" (*Ps.* cvii. 7).

12. OF GOD'S PRESENCE.

As Israel was, so are the saints now, "a people near to Jehovah." He lets not go the hand of a saint for a moment, nor departs from him. His presence goes with him continually. And faith realizes this; a God at hand; ever near; nearer than sin, or Satan, or the world, nearer than self, or the flesh, or any enemy. The perpetual presence of God is the portion and privilege of each one that has tasted that the Lord is gracious.

"My presence shall go with thee" (*Ex.* xxxiii. 14).

" Thou art near, O Lord" (*Ps.* cxix. 151).

" The upright shall dwell in thy presence" (*Ps.* cxl. 13).

" The Lord his God is with him, and the shout of a king is among them" (*Num.* xxiii. 21).

" Fear thou not, for I am with thee" (*Isa.* xli. 10).

" At that day shall ye know that I am in my Father, and ye in me, and I in you. He that hath my commandments, and keepeth them, he it is that loveth me : and he that loveth me shall be loved of my Father, and I will love him, and will manifest myself unto him. Judas saith unto him, not Iscariot, Lord, how is it that thou wilt manifest thyself unto us, and not unto the world ? Jesus answered and said unto him, If a man love me, he will keep my words : and my Father will love him, and we will come unto him, and make our abode with him. He that loveth me not keepeth not my sayings : and the word which ye hear is not mine, but the Father's which sent me" (*John* xiv. 20–24).

13. OF EXEMPTION FROM EVIL.

Not from sorrow, nor sickness, nor pain, is a saint exempted; but from all these, *as evils;* nay, and probably from many sorrows and sicknesses which would otherwise have befallen him. As God when he shut the door of the ark shut out evil as well as shut in Noah and his family, so is it with the believer. From as much of trouble as is consistent with discipline and training he is saved; and all the rest turned into blessing.

"Many are the afflictions of the righteous : but the Lord delivereth him out of them all" (*Ps.* xxxiv. 19).

"There shall no evil happen to the just" (*Prov.* xii. 21).

"He shall not be afraid of evil tidings : his heart is fixed, trusting in the Lord" (*Ps.* cxii. 7).

"He shall deliver thee in six troubles : yea, in seven there shall no evil touch thee. In famine he shall redeem thee from death :

and in war from the power of the sword. Thou shalt be hid from the scourge of the tongue : neither shalt thou be afraid of destruction when it cometh " (*Job* v. 19–21).

" And they thirsted not when he led them through the deserts : he caused the waters to flow out of the rock for them : he clave the rock also, and the waters gushed out " (*Isa.* xlviii. 21).

" The steps of a good man are ordered by the Lord : and he delighteth in his way. Though he fall, he shall not be utterly cast down : for the Lord upholdeth him with his hand. I have been young, and now am old ; yet have I not seen the righteous forsaken, nor his seed begging bread. He is ever merciful, and lendeth ; and his seed is blessed. Depart from evil, and do good ; and dwell for evermore. For the Lord loveth judgment, and forsaketh not his saints ; they are preserved for ever : but the seed of the wicked shall be cut off. The righteous shall inherit the land, and dwell therein for ever. The mouth of the righteous speaketh wisdom, and his tongue talketh of judgment. The law of his God is in his heart; none of his steps shall slide. The wicked watcheth the righteous, and seeketh to slay him. The Lord will not leave him in his hand, nor condemn him when he is judged. Wait on the Lord, and keep his way, and he shall exalt thee to inherit the land : when the wicked are cut off, thou shalt see it. I have seen the wicked in great power, and spreading himself like a green bay tree. Yet he passed away, and, lo, he was not : yea, I sought him, but he could not be found. Mark the perfect man, and behold the upright : for the end of that man is peace " (*Ps.* xxxvii. 23–37).

" The Lord knoweth the days of the upright : and their inheritance shall be for ever. They shall not be ashamed in the evil time : and in the days of famine they shall be satisfied " (*Ps.* xxxvii. 18, 19).

" Whoso hearkeneth unto me shall dwell safely, and shall be quiet from fear of evil " (*Prov.* i. 33).

" Whoso keepeth the commandment shall fear no evil thing" (*Eccles.* viii. 5).

" The fear of the Lord tendeth to life: and he that hath it shall abide satisfied; he shall not be visited with evil" (*Prov.* xix. 23).

" He that dwelleth in the secret place of the most High shall abide under the shadow of the Almighty. I will say of the Lord, He is my refuge and my fortress: my God; in him will I trust. Surely he shall deliver thee from the snare of the fowler, and from the noisome pestilence. He shall cover thee with his feathers, and under his wings shalt thou trust: his truth shall be thy shield and buckler. Thou shalt not be afraid for the terror by night; nor for the arrow that flieth by day; nor for the pestilence that walketh in darkness; nor for the destruction that wasteth at noonday. A thousand shall fall at thy side, and ten thousand at thy right hand; but it shall not come nigh thee. Only with thine eyes shalt thou behold and see the reward of the wicked. Because thou hast made the Lord,

which is my refuge, even the most High,
thy habitation; there shall no evil befall
thee, neither shall any plague come nigh
thy dwelling" (*Ps.* xci. 1–10).

14. OF BLESSING IN TRIAL.

God comforteth us in sorrow. But this is
not all. He bringeth good out of all evil.
He smites the rock and the waters gush forth.
It is not blessing in spite of trial, or blessing
after trial, but blessing *in* trial. He makes
the bitter waters sweet; but, more than this,
he makes the very bitterness to nourish and
heal us.

" As a man chasteneth his son, so the
Lord thy God chasteneth thee" (*Deut.*
viii. 5).

" And if they be bound in fetters, and
be holden in cords of affliction; then he
showeth them their work, and their transgressions that they have exceeded. He
openeth also their ear to discipline, and com-
mandeth that they return from iniquity"
(*Job* xxxvi. 8–10).

" Happy is the man whom God correcteth: therefore despise not thou the chastening of the Almighty: for he maketh sore, and bindeth up; he woundeth, and his hands make whole" (*Job* v. 17, 18).

"Blessed is the man whom thou chastenest, O Lord, and teachest him out of thy law; that thou mayest give him rest from the days of adversity, until the pit be digged for the wicked" (*Ps.* xciv. 12, 13).

"Before I was afflicted I went astray: but now have I kept thy word. It is good for me that I have been afflicted; that I might learn thy statutes. I know, O Lord, that thy judgments are right, and that thou in faithfulness hast afflicted me" (*Ps.* cxix. 67, 71, 75).

"Whom the Lord loveth he correcteth; even as a father the son in whom he delighteth" (*Prov.* iii. 12).

"I will turn my hand upon thee, and purely purge away thy dross" (*Isa.* i. 25).

"For our light affliction, which is but for a moment, worketh for us a far more

exceeding and eternal weight of glory"
(2 *Cor.* iv. 17).

" I know that this shall turn to my salvation through your prayer, and the supply
of the Spirit of Jesus Christ " (*Phil.* i. 19).

" Whom the Lord loveth he chasteneth,
and scourgeth every son whom he receiveth.
If ye endure chastening, God dealeth with
you as with sons; for what son is he whom
the father chasteneth not? They verily
for a few days chastened us after their own
pleasure; but he for our profit, that we
might be partakers of his holiness. Now
no chastening for the present seemeth to be
joyous, but grievous: nevertheless afterward it yieldeth the peaceable fruit of
righteousness unto them which are exer-
cised thereby " (*Heb.* xii. 6, 7, 10, 11).

" As many as I love, I rebuke and
chasten " (*Rev.* iii. 19).

" The trying of your faith worketh
patience. Blessed is the man that endureth
temptation: for when he is tried, he shall
receive the crown of life, which the Lord

hath promised to them that love him" (*James* i. 3, 12).

"And thou shalt remember all the way which the Lord thy God led thee these forty years in the wilderness, to humble thee, and to prove thee, to know what was in thine heart, whether thou wouldest keep his commandments or no. And he humbled thee, and suffered thee to hunger, and fed thee with manna, which thou knewest not, neither did thy fathers know; that he might make thee know that man doth not live by bread only, but by every word that proceedeth out of the mouth of the Lord doth man live. Thy raiment waxed not old upon thee, neither did thy foot swell, these forty years. Thou shalt also consider in thine heart, that as a man chasteneth his son, so the Lord thy God chasteneth thee" (*Deut.* viii. 2–5).

"I have chosen thee in the furnace of affliction" (*Isa.* xlviii. 10).

"I will melt them, and try them" (*Jer.* ix. 7).

"Many shall be purified, and made white, and tried" (*Dan.* xii. 10).

"Tribulation worketh patience" (*Rom.* v. 3).

"We are chastened of the Lord, that we should not be condemned with the world" (1 *Cor.* xi. 32).

"For thou, O God, hast proved us: thou hast tried us, as silver is tried. Thou broughtest us into the net; thou laidst affliction upon our loins. Thou hast caused men to ride over our heads; we went through fire and through water; but thou broughtest us out into a wealthy place" (*Ps.* lxvi. 10–12).

"Beloved, think it not strange concerning the fiery trial which is to try you, as though some strange thing happened unto you: but rejoice, inasmuch as ye are partakers of Christ's sufferings; that, when his glory shall be revealed, ye may be glad also with exceeding joy. If ye be reproached for the name of Christ, happy are ye; for the spirit of glory and of God resteth upon you: on their part he is evil spoken of, but on your part he is glorified " (1 *Pet.* iv. 12–14).

15. OF SATISFACTION.

Not like the men of this world does the believing man wander about, asking "Who will show me any good?" not like them does he hew out broken cisterns that can hold no water; not like them does he spend his money for that which is not bread, and his labour for that which satisfieth not. He eats that which is good, and his soul delights itself in fatness. He is satisfied with the goodness of the Lord. He has not to *seek* happiness; he has *found* it. The bread which he has found in his Father's house is enough and to spare. He has not to go about either to buy or to beg. He is content; he says, It is enough. For a Divine fulness is now his heritage; and out of this Divine fulness his faith daily supplies all wants.

"O Naphtali, satisfied with favour, and full with the blessing of the Lord" (*Deut.* xxxiii. 23).

"The meek shall eat and be satisfied' (*Ps.* xxii. 26).

" They shall be abundantly satisfied with the fatness of thy house " (*Ps.* xxxvi. 8).

" My people shall be satisfied with my goodness, saith the Lord" (*Jer.* xxxi. 14).

" O God, thou art my God; early will I seek thee: my soul thirsteth for thee, my flesh longeth for thee in a dry and thirsty land, where no water is. To see thy power and thy glory, so as I have seen thee in the sanctuary. Because thy lovingkindness is better than life, my lips shall praise thee. Thus will I bless thee while I live: I will lift up my hands in thy name. My soul shall be satisfied as with marrow and fatness; and my mouth shall praise thee with joyful lips: when I remember thee upon my bed, and meditate on thee in the night watches. Because thou hast been my help, therefore in the shadow of thy wings will I rejoice " (*Ps.* lxiii. 1–7).

" The fear of the Lord tendeth to life: and he that hath it shall abide satisfied; he shall not be visited with evil" (*Prov.* xix. 23).

" Blessed is the man whom thou choosest,

and causest to approach unto thee, that he may dwell in thy courts: we shall be satisfied with the goodness of thy house, even of thy holy temple" (*Ps.* lxv. 4).

"The Lord is my shepherd; I shall not want. He maketh me to lie down in green pastures: he leadeth me beside the still waters. He restoreth my soul: he leadeth me in the paths of righteousness for his name's sake. Yea, though I walk through the valley of the shadow of death, I will fear no evil: for thou art with me; thy rod and thy staff they comfort me. Thou preparest a table before me in the presence of mine enemies: thou anointest my head with oil; my cup runneth over. Surely goodness and mercy shall follow me all the days of my life: and I will dwell in the house of the Lord for ever" (*Ps.* xxiii.).

"Bless the Lord, O my soul: and all that is within me, bless his holy name. Bless the Lord, O my soul, and forget not all his benefits: who forgiveth all thine iniquities; who healeth all thy diseases; who redeemeth thy life from destruction;

who crowneth thee with lovingkindness
and tender mercies; who satisfieth thy
mouth with good things; so that thy youth
is renewed like the eagle's. The Lord
executeth righteousness and judgment for
all that are oppressed. He made known
his ways unto Moses, his acts unto the
children of Israel" (*Ps.* ciii. 1–7).

16. OF GRACE.

In general "grace" means God's "free
love," or "favour;" though sometimes it may
mean the power put forth by that free love in
the soul ; and sometimes the effects of that
power in the changes wrought in the soul.
Without defining the meaning in individual
passages, we quote a few in which this "grace"
is promised.

" By grace are ye saved" (*Eph.* ii. 8).

" A good man obtaineth favour of the
Lord" (*Prov.* xii. 2).

" My grace is sufficient for thee: for my
strength is made perfect in weakness"
(2 *Cor.* xii. 9).

" I will be gracious to whom I will be

gracious, and will show mercy on whom I will show mercy" (*Ex.* xxxiii. 19).

"Of his fulness have all we received, and grace for grace. For the law was given by Moses, but grace and truth came by Jesus Christ" (*John* i. 16).

"A God ready to pardon, gracious and merciful, slow to anger, and of great kindness" (*Neh.* ix. 17).

"Ye know the grace of our Lord Jesus Christ" (2 *Cor.* viii. 9).

"Let us come boldly unto the throne of grace, that we may obtain mercy, and find grace to help in time of need" (*Heb.* iv. 16).

"The grace of the Lord Jesus Christ, and the love of God, and the communion of the Holy Ghost, be with you all" (2 *Cor.* xiii. 14).

"Noah found grace in the eyes of the Lord" (*Gen.* vi. 8).

"Satisfied with favour, and full with the blessing of the Lord" (*Deut.* xxxiii. 23).

"The Lord will give grace and glory: no good thing will he withhold from them that walk uprightly" (*Ps.* lxxxiv. 11).

"Therefore will the Lord wait, that he may be gracious unto you, and therefore will he be exalted, that he may have mercy upon you" (*Isa.* xxx. 18).

"Grace be unto you, and peace, from him which is, and which was, and which is to come" (*Rev.* i. 4).

"Where sin abounded, grace did much more abound" (*Rom.* v. 20).

"The grace of our Lord was exceeding abundant with faith and love which is in Christ Jesus" (1 *Tim.* i. 14).

"God is able to make all grace abound toward you" (2 *Cor.* ix. 8).

"Be strong in the grace that is in Christ Jesus" (2 *Tim.* ii. 1).

"Let us have grace, whereby we may serve God acceptably with reverence and godly fear" (*Heb.* xii. 28).

17. Of Divine Teaching.

Our training for the kingdom is Divine. It is conducted by God himself. Our education is in his hands, not in our own, nor in human hands. The whole discipline through which we are passing is Divine. God is our teacher. Our instruction must be perfect, seeing our instructor is Divine. Discipleship, under such a master, must be blessed.

" The same anointing teacheth you of all things " (1 *John* ii. 27).

" I am the Lord thy God which teacheth thee to profit " (*Isa.* xlviii. 17).

" Behold, God exalteth by his power; who teacheth like him?" (*Job* xxxvi. 22).

" Blessed be the Lord my strength, which teacheth my hands to war, and my fingers to fight " (*Ps.* cxliv. 1).

" Blessed is the man whom thou teachest " (*Ps.* xciv. 12).

" Teach me to do thy will; for thou art my God " (*Ps.* cxliii. 10).

" The Comforter, which is the Holy Ghost, whom the Father will send in my name, he shall teach you all things, and bring all things to your remembrance, whatsoever I have said unto you " (*John* xiv. 26).

" Show me thy ways, O Lord; teach me thy paths. Lead me in thy truth, and

teach me: for thou art the God of my salvation; on thee do I wait all the day.
Remember, O Lord, thy tender mercies and
thy lovingkindnesses; for they have been
ever of old.   Remember not the sins of my
youth, nor my transgressions: according to
thy mercy remember thou me for thy goodness' sake, O Lord.   Good and upright is
the Lord: therefore will he teach sinners in
the way.   The meek will he guide in judgment: and the meek will he teach his way.
All the paths of the Lord are mercy and
truth unto such as keep his covenant and
his testimonies.   For thy name's sake, O
Lord, pardon mine iniquity; for it is great.
What man is he that feareth the Lord? him
shall he teach in the way that he shall
choose.   His soul shall dwell at ease; and
his seed shall inherit the earth.   The secret
of the Lord is with them that fear him;
and he will show them his covenant "
(*Ps.* xxv. 4–14).

"I will instruct thee and teach thee in
the way which thou shalt go: I will guide
thee with mine eye " (*Ps.* xxxii. 8).

" The Dayspring from on high hath visited us, to give light to them that sit in darkness and in the shadow of death, to guide our feet into the way of peace" (*Luke* i. 78, 79).

" If any man will do his will, he shall know of the doctrine, whether it be of God, or whether I speak of myself" (*John* vii. 17).

" It is written in the prophets, And they shall be all taught of God. Every man therefore that hath heard, and hath learned of the Father, cometh unto me" (*John* vi. 45).

" O God, thou hast taught me from my youth" (*Ps.* lxxi. 17).

" All thy children shall be taught of the Lord" (*Isa.* liv. 13).

18. OF THE HOLY SPIRIT'S HELP.

The great helper of the saint is the Holy Ghost. Through him he was first enabled to believe, and by him he was filled, after believing; for through faith we receive the promised Spirit. Such is the power of evil, within and without, that nothing short of Omnipotence can bring him safely through.

The Holy Spirit dwells in him and works in him ; and thus he is carried forward against every enemy and every obstacle, overcoming all, through the Almighty helper.

" The love of God is shed abroad in our hearts by the Holy Ghost which is given unto us" (*Rom.* v. 5).

" He shall give you another Comforter, that he may abide with you for ever ; even the Spirit of truth" (*John* xiv. 16, 17).

" The Holy Ghost which dwelleth in us" (2 *Tim.* i. 14).

" We have received, not the spirit of the world, but the spirit which is of God" (1 *Cor.* ii. 12).

" That we might receive the promise of the Spirit through faith" (*Gal.* iii. 14).

" The Holy Ghost shall teach you" (*Luke* xii. 12).

"God hath revealed them unto us by his Spirit" (1 *Cor.* ii. 10).

" When he, the Spirit of truth, is come, he will guide you into all truth" (*John* xvi. 13).

"Grieve not the Holy Spirit of God,

whereby ye are sealed unto the day of redemption" (*Eph.* iv. 30).

"He that believeth on me, out of his belly shall flow rivers of living water. But this spake he of the Spirit, which they that believe on him should receive" (*John* vii. 38, 39).

"But the anointing which ye have received of him abideth in you, and ye need not that any man teach you: but as the same anointing teacheth you of all things, and is truth, and is no lie, and even as it hath taught you, ye shall abide in him" (1 *John* ii. 27).

"Behold, I will pour out my Spirit unto you, I will make known my words unto you" (*Prov.* i. 23).

"Until the Spirit be poured upon us from on high, and the wilderness be a fruitful field" (*Isa.* xxxii. 15).

"This is my covenant with them, saith the Lord; My Spirit that is upon thee, and my words which I have put in thy mouth, shall not depart out of thy mouth, nor out of the mouth of thy seed, nor out of the mouth of thy seed's seed, saith the Lord, from henceforth and for ever " (*Isa.* lix. 21).

" I will put my Spirit within you, and cause you to walk in my statutes, and ye shall keep my judgments, and do them" (*Ezek.* xxxvi. 27).

" If ye then, being evil, know how to give good gifts unto your children; how much more shall your heavenly Father give the Holy Spirit to them that ask him?" (*Luke* xi. 13.)

" I will pour upon the house of David, and upon the inhabitants of Jerusalem, the spirit of grace and of supplications " (*Zech.* xii. 10).

" Ye have received the Spirit of adoption, whereby we cry, Abba, Father. The Spirit also helpeth our infirmities: for we know not what we should pray for as we ought: but the Spirit itself maketh intercession for us with groanings which cannot be uttered. And he that searcheth the hearts knoweth what is the mind of the Spirit, because he maketh intercession for the saints according to the will of God" (*Rom.* viii. 15, 26, 27).

" Because ye are sons, God hath sent forth the Spirit of his Son into your hearts, crying, Abba, Father" (*Gal.* iv. 6).

19. OF LIFE.

It is not *one* impartation of life that will suffice for us, there must be a daily, hourly influx, an influx as constant as that of the light. We need fresh air every moment for our bodies; so do we need the vital air of heaven, the life of Christ, for our souls. Constant believing, constant abiding, constant trusting; and, as the result of these, constant life. It is not merely the promise of a life at the moment of believing, or of a life at the close of this mortal condition here, but of a life all through, a daily, hourly life, through infusion every moment of something from above by the power of the Holy Ghost.

" Thou wilt show me the path of life" (*Ps.* xvi. 11).

" With thee is the fountain of life" (*Ps.* xxxvi. 9).

" In him was life; and the life was the light of men" (*John* i. 4).

" Verily, verily, I say unto you, He that believeth on me hath everlasting life. I am that bread of life. Your fathers did eat manna in the wilderness, and are dead. This is the bread which cometh down from heaven, that a man may eat thereof, and not die. I am the living bread which came down from heaven: if any man eat of this bread, he shall live for ever: and the bread that I will give is my flesh, which I will give for the life of the world. The Jews therefore strove among themselves, saying, How can this man give us his flesh to eat? Then Jesus said unto them, Verily, verily, I say unto you, Except ye eat the flesh of the Son of man, and drink his blood, ye have no life in you. Whoso eateth my flesh, and drinketh my blood, hath eternal life; and I will raise him up at the last day. For my flesh is meat indeed, and my blood is drink indeed. He that eateth my flesh, and drinketh my blood, dwelleth in me, and I in him. As the living Father hath sent me, and I live by the Father: so he that eateth me, even he shall live by me. This is that bread which came down from heaven: not as your fathers did eat manna, and are dead: he that eateth of this bread shall live for ever " (*John* vi. 47–58).

" Always bearing about in the body the dying of the Lord Jesus, that the life also of Jesus might be made manifest in our body. For we which live are alway delivered unto death for Jesus' sake, that the life also of Jesus might be made manifest in our mortal flesh. So then death worketh in us, but life in you" (2 *Cor.* iv. 10–12).

" For I through the law am dead to the law, that I might live unto God. I am crucified with Christ: nevertheless I live; yet not I, but Christ liveth in me: and the life which I now live in the flesh I live by the faith of the Son of God, who loved me, and gave himself for me" (*Gal.* ii. 19, 20).

" For ye are dead, and your life is hid with Christ in God. When Christ, who is our life, shall appear, then shall ye also appear with him in glory" (*Col.* iii. 3, 4).

" And this is the record, that God hath

given to us eternal life; and this life is in his Son. He that hath the Son hath life; and he that hath not the Son of God hath not life. These things have I written unto you that believe on the name of the Son of God, that ye may know that ye have eternal life, and that ye may believe on the name of the Son of God" (1 *John* v. 11–13).

"To whom coming, as unto a living stone, disallowed indeed of men, but chosen of God, and precious, ye also, as lively stones, are built up a spiritual house, an holy priesthood, to offer up spiritual sacrifices, acceptable to God by Jesus Christ" (1 *Pet.* ii. 4, 5).

"For though he was crucified through weakness, yet he liveth by the power of God. For we also are weak in him, but we shall live with him by the power of God toward you" (2 *Cor.* xiii. 4).

"Now if we be dead with Christ, we believe that we shall also live with him: knowing that Christ being raised from the dead dieth no more; death hath no more dominion over him. For in that he died, he died unto sin once; but in that he liveth, he liveth unto God. Likewise reckon ye also yourselves to be dead indeed unto sin, but alive unto God through Jesus Christ our Lord. Let not sin therefore reign in your mortal body, that ye should obey it in the lusts thereof. Neither yield ye your members as instruments of unrighteousness unto sin: but yield yourselves unto God, as those that are alive from the dead, and your members as instruments of righteousness unto God" (*Rom.* vi. 8–13).

"The last Adam was made a quickening spirit" (1 *Cor.* xv. 45).

"Because I live, ye shall live also" (*John* xiv. 19).

20. OF FRUIT-BEARING.

As God's olive-trees, we are to bear fruit; as fig-trees planted in a vineyard, we are to bear the best of fruit; as his palms, we are to continue fruitful to the last. Our sap and vigour for fruit-bearing is to be derived from him with whom we are connected—Jesus Christ, our living root and stem. Our lives are to be all ever laden with fruit, bearing fruit not only every month, but every day and hour.

"I am the true vine, and my Father is the husbandman. Every branch in me that beareth not fruit he taketh away; and every branch that beareth fruit he purgeth it, that it may bring forth more fruit. Now ye are clean through the word which I have spoken unto you. Abide in me, and I in you. As the branch cannot bear fruit of itself, except it abide in the vine; no more can ye, except ye abide in me. I am the vine, ye are the branches: he that abideth in me, and I in him, the same bringeth forth much fruit; for without me ye can do nothing. If a man abide not in me, he is cast forth as a branch, and is withered; and men gather them, and cast them into the fire, and they are burned. If ye abide in me, and my words abide in you, ye shall ask what ye will, and it shall be done unto you. Herein is my Father glorified, that ye bear much fruit; so shall ye be my disciples" (*John* xv. 1–8).

" Blessed is the man that walketh not in the counsel of the ungodly, nor standeth in the way of sinners, nor sitteth in the seat of the scornful: but his delight is in the law of the Lord; and in his law doth he meditate day and night. And he shall be like a tree planted by the rivers of water, that bringeth forth his fruit in his season: his leaf also shall not wither; and whatsoever he doeth shall prosper" (*Ps.* i. 1–3).

" Blessed is the man that trusteth in the Lord, and whose hope the Lord is: for he shall be as a tree planted by the waters, and that spreadeth out her roots by the river, and shall not see when heat cometh, but her leaf shall be green; and shall not be careful in the year of drought, neither shall cease from yielding fruit" (*Jer.* xvii. 7, 8).

" The righteous shall flourish like the palm-tree; he shall grow like a cedar in Lebanon. Those that be planted in the house of the Lord shall flourish in the courts of our God. They shall still bring forth fruit in old age; they shall be fat and flourishing; to show that the Lord is upright:

he is my rock, and there is no unrighteousness in him " (*Ps.* xcii. 12–15).

" But the fruit of the Spirit is love, joy, peace, long-suffering, gentleness, goodness, faith, meekness, temperance : against such there is no law.   And they that are Christ's have crucified the flesh with the affections and lusts" (*Gal.* v. 22–24).

" For ye were sometimes darkness, but now are ye light in the Lord : walk as children of light : (for the fruit of the Spirit is in all goodness and righteousness and truth;) proving what is acceptable unto the Lord.   And have no fellowship with the unfruitful works of darkness, but rather reprove them " (*Eph.* v. 8–11).

" But the wisdom that is from above is first pure, then peaceable, gentle, and easy to be entreated, full of mercy and good fruits, without partiality, and without hypocrisy. And the fruit of righteousness is sown in peace of them that make peace" (*James* iii. 17, 18).

" Put on therefore, as the elect of God,

holy and beloved, bowels of mercies, kindness, humbleness of mind, meekness, longsuffering ; forbearing one another, and forgiving one another, if any man have a quarrel against any: even as Christ forgave you, so also do ye. And above all these things put on charity, which is the bond of perfectness" (*Col.* iii. 12, 13).

" For this cause we also, since the day we heard it, do not cease to pray for you, and to desire that ye might be filled with the knowledge of his will in all wisdom and spiritual understanding ; that ye might walk worthy of the Lord unto all pleasing, being fruitful in every good work, and increasing in the knowledge of God" (*Col.* i. 9, 10).

" Wherefore, my brethren, ye also are become dead to the law by the body of Christ; that ye should be married to another, even to him who is raised from the dead, that we should bring forth fruit unto God " (*Rom.* vii. 4).

" I speak after the manner of men because of the infirmity of your flesh: for as ye have yielded your members servants to uncleanness and to iniquity unto iniquity; even so now yield your members servants to right-eousness unto holiness. For when ye were the servants of sin, ye were free from right-eousness. What fruit had ye then in those things whereof ye are now ashamed? for the end of those things is death. But now be-ing made free from sin, and become servants to God, ye have your fruit unto holiness, and the end everlasting life" (*Rom.* vi. 19–22).

21. OF ANGELIC SERVICE.

Often have angels visited the earth; in early days their visits were not so "far between" as in later times. They came as messengers; as inflictors of wrath on the enemy; as de-fenders and helpers of the saints. Though invisible now, they still carry on their work of love and power in behalf of the heirs of salvation.

" The angel of the Lord encampeth round about them that fear him, and delivereth them " (*Ps.* xxxiv. 7).

" He shall give his angels charge over thee, to keep thee in all thy ways; they shall bear thee up in their hands, lest thou dash thy foot against a stone" (*Ps.* xci. 11, 12).

"The Lord hath sent his angel, and hath delivered me out of the hand of Herod" (*Acts* xii. 11).

"Are they not all ministering spirits, sent forth to minister for them who shall be heirs of salvation?" (*Heb.* i. 14.)

"I saw four angels standing on the four corners of the earth, holding the four winds of the earth, that the wind should not blow on the earth, nor on the sea, nor on any tree. And I saw another angel ascending from the east, having the seal of the living God: and he cried with a loud voice to the four angels, to whom it was given to hurt the earth and the sea, saying, Hurt not the earth, neither the sea, nor the trees, till we have sealed the servants of our God in their foreheads" (*Rev.* vii. 1–3).

"I say unto you, That in heaven their angels do always behold the face of my Father which is in heaven" (*Matt.* xviii. 10).

22. OF RESURRECTION.

In one sense we are, according to the Apostle, already risen with Christ. When he died we died ; when he rose we rose. " Risen with Christ" is the Apostle's description of the brethren at Colosse (Col. iii. 1). But there is the actual resurrection of the body in prospect. We shall arise, and become immortal. Disease, pain, death, shall have no more dominion over us.

" Thou shalt be recompensed at the resurrection of the just" (*Luke* xiv. 14).

" Thy dead men shall live, together with my dead body shall they arise. Awake and sing, ye that dwell in dust : for thy dew is as the dew of herbs, and the earth shall cast out the dead" (*Isa*. xxvi. 19).

" He will swallow up death in victory" (*Isa*. xxv. 8).

" God will redeem my soul from the power of the grave" (*Ps*. xlix. 15).

" God hath both raised up the Lord, and will also raise up us by his own power" (1 *Cor*. vi. 14).

" Blessed and holy is he that hath part in the first resurrection " (*Rev.* xx. 6).

" Whoso eateth my flesh, and drinketh my blood, hath eternal life; and I will raise him up at the last day " (*John* vi. 54).

" But God, who is rich in mercy, for his great love wherewith he loved us, even when we were dead in sins, hath quickened us together with Christ, (by grace ye are saved;) and hath raised us up together, and made us sit together in heavenly places in Christ Jesus " (*Eph.* ii. 4–6).

" Buried with him in baptism, wherein also ye are risen with him through the faith of the operation of God, who hath raised him from the dead. And you, being dead in your sins and the uncircumcision of your flesh, hath he quickened together with him, having forgiven you all trespasses " (*Col.* ii. 12, 13).

" As the waters fail from the sea, and the flood decayeth and drieth up ; so man lieth down, and riseth not: till the heavens be no more, they shall not awake, nor be raised out of their sleep. O that thou wouldest hide me in the grave, that thou wouldest keep me secret, until thy wrath be past, that thou wouldest appoint me a set time, and remember me ! If a man die, shall he live again? all the days of my appointed time will I wait, till my change come. Thou shalt call, and I will answer thee : thou wilt have a desire to the work of thine hands " (*Job* xiv. 11–15).

" But they which shall be accounted worthy to obtain that world, and the resurrection from the dead, neither marry, nor are given in marriage : neither can they die any more : for they are equal unto the angels ; and are the children of God, being the children of the resurrection. Now that the dead are raised, even Moses showed at the bush, when he calleth the Lord the God of Abraham, and the God of Isaac, and the God of Jacob. For he is not a God of the dead, but of the living " (*Luke* xx. 35–38).

" For our conversation is in heaven ; from whence also we look for the Saviour, the Lord Jesus Christ : who shall change our vile body, that it may be fashioned like unto his glorious body, according to the working whereby he is able even to subdue all things unto himself" (*Phil.* iii. 20, 21).

"But some man will say, How are the dead raised up? and with what body do they come? Thou fool, that which thou sowest is not quickened, except it die: and that which thou sowest, thou sowest not that body that shall be, but bare grain, it may chance of wheat, or of some other grain: but God giveth it a body as it hath pleased him, and to every seed his own body. All flesh is not the same flesh: but there is one kind of flesh of men, another flesh of beasts, another of fishes, and another of birds. There are also celestial bodies, and bodies terrestrial: but the glory of the celestial is one, and the glory of the terrestrial is another. There is one glory of the sun, and another glory of the moon, and another glory of the stars: for one star differeth from another star in glory. So also is the resurrection of the dead. It is sown in corruption; it is raised in incorruption: it is sown in dishonour; it is raised in glory: it is sown in weaknesss; it is raised in power: it is sown a natural body; it is raised a spiritual body. There is a natural body, and there is a spiritual body. And so it is written, The first man Adam was made a living soul; the last Adam was made a quickening spirit" (1 *Cor.* xv. 35-45).

"Behold, I show you a mystery; We shall not all sleep, but we shall all be changed, in a moment, in the twinkling of an eye, at the last trump: for the trumpet shall sound, and the dead shall be raised incorruptible, and we shall be changed. For this corruptible must put on incorruption, and this mortal must put on immortality. So when this corruptible shall have put on incorruption, and this mortal shall have put on immortality, then shall be brought to pass the saying that is written, Death is swallowed up in victory. O death, where is thy sting? O grave, where is thy victory? The sting of death is sin; and the strength of sin is the law. But thanks be to God, which giveth us the victory through our Lord Jesus Christ" (1 *Cor.* xv. 51-57).

" But I would not have you to be ignorant, brethren, concerning them which are
asleep, that ye sorrow not, even as others
which have no hope. For if we believe that
Jesus died and rose again, even so them also
which sleep in Jesus will God bring with
him. For this we say unto you by the
word of the Lord, that we which are alive
and remain unto the coming of the Lord
shall not prevent them which are asleep.
For the Lord himself shall descend from
heaven with a shout, with the voice of the
archangel, and with the trump of God: and
the dead in Christ shall rise first: then we
which are alive and remain shall be caught
up together with them in the clouds, to meet
the Lord in the air: and so shall we ever be
with the Lord. Wherefore comfort one
another with these words " (1 *Thess.* iv. 13–
18).

23. OF VICTORY.

We conquer because Christ has conquered.
His victory is ours. He fought for us; he
overcame for us. His foes are ours; and he
will not leave one of them in possession of

the battle-field. Their strength and numbers are nothing to him. Every enemy shall be put under his feet and ours. Let us not fear the adversary; yet let us watch, and let us fight. However many the battles may be, however hard the struggle, we are sure of victory. He has promised it!

"In all these things we are more than conquerors through him that loved us" (*Rom.* viii. 37).

"Thanks be to God, which giveth us the victory through our Lord Jesus Christ" (1 *Cor.* xv. 57).

"Whatsoever is born of God overcometh the world: and this is the victory that overcometh the world, even our faith. Who is he that overcometh the world, but he that believeth that Jesus is the Son of God?" (1 *John* v. 4, 5.)

"They overcame him by the blood of the Lamb, and by the word of their testimony" (*Rev.* xii. 11).

"Finally, my brethren, be strong in the Lord, and in the power of his might. Put on the whole armour of God, that ye may be able to stand against the wiles of the devil. For we wrestle not against flesh and blood, but against principalities, against powers, against the rulers of the darkness of this world, against spiritual wickedness in high places. Wherefore take unto you the whole armour of God, that ye may be able to withstand in the evil day, and having done all, to stand. Stand therefore, having your loins girt about with truth, and having on the breastplate of righteousness ; and your feet shod with the preparation of the gospel of peace ; above all, taking the shield of faith, wherewith ye shall be able to quench all the fiery darts of the wicked. And take the helmet of salvation, and the sword of the Spirit, which is the word of God : praying always with all prayer and supplication in the Spirit, and watching thereunto with all perseverance and supplication for all saints " (*Eph.* vi. 10–18).

" He that overcometh shall inherit all things ; and I will be his God, and he shall be my son " (*Rev.* xxi. 7).

24. OF DOMINION.

Christ shares his power with his people; and they are heirs of the royalty which belongs to him. At present they are obscure and weak; hereafter they are to sit upon a throne as God's royal priesthood. For that which belongs to the head belongs to the members also.

"To him that overcometh will I give power over the nations: and he shall rule them with a rod of iron; as the vessels of a potter shall they be broken to shivers: even as I received of my Father" (*Rev*. ii. 26).

"To him that overcometh will I grant to sit with me in my throne, even as I also overcame, and am set down with my Father in his throne" (*Rev*. iii. 21).

"And Jesus said unto them, Verily I say unto you, That ye which have followed me, in the regeneration when the Son of man shall sit in the throne of his glory, ye also shall sit upon twelve thrones, judging the twelve tribes of Israel" (*Matt*. xix. 28).

"Do ye not know that the saints shall

judge the world? and if the world shall be judged by you, are ye unworthy to judge the smallest matters? Know ye not that we shall judge angels?" (1 *Cor*. vi. 2, 3.)

"But ye are a chosen generation, a royal priesthood, an holy nation, a peculiar people; that ye should show forth the praises of him who hath called you out of darkness into his marvellous light" (1 *Pet*. ii. 9).

"And they sung a new song, saying Thou art worthy to take the book, and to open the seals thereof: for thou wast slain, and hast redeemed us to God by thy blood out of every kindred, and tongue, and people, and nation; and hast made us unto our God kings and priests: and we shall reign on the earth" (*Rev*. v. 9, 10).

"And hath made us kings and priests unto God and his Father" (*Rev*. i. 6).

"And I saw thrones, and they sat upon them, and judgment was given unto them: and I saw the souls of them that were beheaded for the witness of Jesus, and for the word of God, and which had not worshipped the beast, neither his image, neither had received his mark upon their foreheads, or in their hands; and they lived and reigned with Christ a thousand years. But the rest of the dead lived not again until the thousand years were finished. This is the first resurrection. Blessed and holy is he that hath part in the first resurrection: on such the second death hath no power, but they shall be priests of God and of Christ, and shall reign with him a thousand years" (*Rev.* xx. 4–6).

" Let the saints be joyful in glory: let them sing aloud upon their beds. Let the high praises of God be in their mouth, and a two-edged sword in their hand; to execute vengeance upon the heathen, and punishments upon the people; to bind their kings with chains, and their nobles with fetters of iron; to execute upon them the judgment written: this honour have all his saints. Praise ye the Lord" (*Ps.* cxlix. 5–9).

25. OF GLORY.

Glory is the essence of all that is excellent, and blessed, and beautiful, and holy; like

the precious ointment of the tabernacle, made
up of many ingredients It is something
which cannot be described ; but that which
God calls by such a word must be something
very precious.   There is one glory of the sun,
and another glory of the stars ; so there is a
glory of the soul, and a glory of the body, and
a glory of this earth, which was given to man
for his habitation.   The glory has for a season
been lost ; sin marred it ; but it shall be seen
again.   There is glory in reserve for Christ ;
glory for the church ; glory for each saint ;
and glory for the city which is to be his
dwelling.

"Thou shalt afterwards receive me to
glory" (*Ps.* lxxiii. 24).

"Let the saints be joyful in glory" (*Ps.*
cxlix. 5).

"The wise shall inherit glory" (*Prov.* iii.
35).

"And the glory which thou gavest me I
have given them ; that they may be one,
even as we are one : I in them, and thou in
me, that they may be made perfect in one ;
and that the world may know that thou
hast sent me, and hast loved them, as thou

hast loved me. Father, I will that they also, whom thou hast given me, be with me where I am; that they may behold my glory, which thou hast given me: for thou lovedst me before the foundation of the world" (*John* xvii. 22–24).

" The glory which shall be revealed in us" (*Rom.* viii. 18).

" But we all, with open face beholding as in a glass the glory of the Lord, are changed into the same image from glory to glory, even as by the Spirit of the Lord" (2 *Cor.* iii. 18).

" Christ in you, the hope of glory " (*Col.* i. 27).

" When Christ, who is our life, shall appear, then shall ye also appear with him in glory " (*Col.* iii. 4).

" Whereunto he called you by our gospel, to the obtaining of the glory of our Lord Jesus Christ " (2 *Thess.* ii. 14).

" Wherein ye greatly rejoice, though now for a season, if need be, ye are in heaviness through manifold temptations : that the trial of your faith, being much more precious than of gold that perisheth, though it be tried with fire, might be found unto praise and honour and glory at the appearing of Jesus Christ: whom having not seen, ye love ; in whom, though now ye see him not, yet believing, ye rejoice with joy unspeakable and full of glory: receiving the end of your faith, even the salvation of your souls. Of which salvation the prophets have enquired and searched diligently, who prophesied of the grace that should come unto you: searching what, or what manner of time the Spirit of Christ which was in them did signify, when it testified beforehand the sufferings of Christ, and the glory that should follow" (1 *Pet.* i. 6–11).

" But we see Jesus, who was made a little lower than the angels for the suffering of death, crowned with glory and honour ; that he by the grace of God should taste death for every man. For it became him, for whom are all things, and by whom are all things, in bringing many sons unto glory, to make the Captain of their salvation

perfect through sufferings. For both he that
sanctifieth and they who are sanctified are all
of one : for which cause he is not ashamed
to call them brethren " (*Heb.* ii. 9–11).

" Remember that Jesus Christ of the seed
of David was raised from the dead according to my gospel : wherein I suffer trouble,
as an evil doer, even unto bonds ; but the
word of God is not bound. Therefore I
endure all things for the elect's sakes, that
they may also obtain the salvation which is
in Christ Jesus with eternal glory. It is a
faithful saying : For if we be dead with him,
we shall also live with him : if we suffer, we
shall also reign with him " (2 *Tim.* ii. 8–12).

" For our light affliction, which is but for
a moment, worketh for us a far more exceeding and eternal weight of glory ; while we
look not at the things which are seen, but at
the things which are not seen : for the things
which are seen are temporal ; but the things
which are not seen are eternal " (2 *Cor.* iv.
17, 18).

CHAPTER III.

FOR THE CHURCH.

THE Greek word which we translate "church" is well known in the Old Testament; as in Ps. xxii. 22, "in the midst of the congregation ('church,' Heb. ii. 11, 12) will I praise thee;" in Ps. xxxv. 18, "I will give thee thanks in the great congregation ('the great church'): I will praise thee among much people;" Ps. xl. 10, "I have not concealed thy lovingkindness and thy truth from the great congregation ('the great church');" Ps. cxlix. 1, "Sing unto the Lord a new song, and his praise in the congregation of the saints ('the church of the saints')."

Hence, in his address to the Sanhedrim, Stephen takes up the word, and speaks of "the church in the wilderness" (Acts vii. 38).

The church, then, is the whole body of saints called out of the race of Adam, chosen in Christ, according to the Father's eternal purpose, and delivered from a present evil world. It is the one spiritual house or temple which God has been building of living stones from the beginning (1 Cor. iii. 16; 1 Pet. ii. 5); the one vine, of which all believers are the branches (John xv. 5); the one loaf, of which all believers are the crumbs (1 Cor. x. 17); the one family or household, of which all believers are the members (Gal. vi. 10; Eph. ii. 19); the one body, of which all believers are the parts and limbs and organs (Eph. iv. 16), and regarding which Paul says, " Christ loved the church, and gave himself for it " (Eph. v. 25, 26).

This is the church to which so many promises are made, and of which such glorious things are spoken. This is the church to which every saint belongs; which sings on earth the song, " Unto him that loved us, and washed us from our sins in his own blood, and hath made us kings and priests unto God and his Father; to him be glory and dominion for ever and ever " (Rev. i. 5, 6); and which sings in heaven, " Thou wast slain, and hast redeemed us to God by thy blood out of every kindred, and tongue, and people, and nation; and hast made us unto our God kings and priests : and we shall reign on the earth " (Rev. v. 9, 10).

Many of the promises to individual saints apply to the church as a whole, and many of the promises to the church are the legitimate property of individual saints.   Let us select a few which best suit the church as a whole.

1. CHRIST'S PRESENCE.

There are two ways in which Christ's nearness to his church is spoken of, two figures by which it is shadowed forth: the one is our being in him, and the other is his being in us; the one our going up to him, and being seated with him in heavenly places; the other his coming down to us, and making his dwelling here: "Lo, I am with you alway, even unto the end of the world."

This presence need not always be visible, but it must be real and vital.   Our life is hid with Christ in God; and his words to us are, "Because I live, ye shall live also."

There must be communication, unbroken communication, between us and the Lord; all the evil in us passing out of us, and all the good in him passing into us.   His fulness is the fountain-head, and from it the streams gush forth on every side.   He comes into his dwelling, into his temple, into his garden; he walks among his candlesticks, and holdeth the seven stars in his right hand.   His Godhead makes all this sure to us.   He is in the midst of us; he breathes on us; he touches us; he sups with us, and we with him.

" At that day ye shall know that I am in my Father, and ye in me, and I in you" (*John* xiv. 20).

" Abide in me, and I in you" (*John* xv. 4).

" In the midst of the seven candlesticks one like unto the Son of man" (*Rev.* i. 13).

" I in them, and thou in me" (*John* xvii. 23).

" He is the head of the body, the church" (*Col.* i. 18).

" Christ as a son over his own house; whose house are we, if we hold fast the confidence and the rejoicing of the hope firm unto the end" (*Heb.* iii. 6).

" Hereby know we that we dwell in him, and he in us, because he hath given us of his Spirit" (1 *John* iv. 13).

" In the midst of the throne, and of the four beasts, and in the midst of the elders, stood a Lamb as it had been slain" (*Rev.* . 6).

" To whom coming, as unto a living stone, disallowed indeed of men, but chosen of God, and precious, ye also, as lively stones, are built up a spiritual house, an holy priesthood, to offer up spiritual sacrifices, acceptable to God by Jesus Christ" (1 *Pet*. ii. 4, 5).

"The king hath brought me into his chambers" (*Cant*. i. 4).

"I am come into my garden, my sister, my spouse" (*Cant*. v. 1).

"Where two or three are gathered together in my name, there am I in the midst of them" (*Matt*. xviii. 20).

"Lo, I am with you alway, even unto the end of the world" (*Matt*. xxviii. 20).

"These things saith he that holdeth the seven stars in his right hand, who walketh in the midst of the seven golden candlesticks" (*Rev*. ii. 1).

2. CHRIST'S GRACE.

The grace or free love of Christ is the sunshine in which the church walks, and without which she stumbles and strays. For his church the large fountain of his grace has been opened, and is flowing still.

" Ye know the grace of our Lord Jesus Christ " (2 *Cor.* viii. 9).

" The grace of our Lord Jesus Christ be with you all " (*Rev.* xxii. 21).

" Grace be unto you from Jesus Christ, the faithful witness, the first begotten of the dead, and the Prince of the kings of the earth " (*Rev.* i. 4, 5).

" The grace of our Lord Jesus Christ be with you " (*Rom.* xvi. 20).

3. CHRIST'S POWER.

All power is given unto him in heaven and in earth, and it is this omnipotence that is at work in behalf of his church. It is this that is the church's shield and weapon. Encircled with this and upheld by this she is safe ; nay, she conquers ; nay, she is more than conqueror, through him that loved her.

" On this rock will I build my church; and the gates of hell shall not prevail against it " (*Matt.* xvi. 18).

" Who shall separate us from the love of Christ? shall tribulation, or distress, or per-secution, or famine, or nakedness, or peril, or sword? Nay, in all these things we are more than conquerors through him that loved us. For I am persuaded, that neither death, nor life, nor angels, nor principalities, nor powers, nor things present, nor things to come, nor height, nor depth, nor any other creature, shall be able to separate us from the love of God, which is in Christ Jesus our Lord" (*Rom.* viii. 35–39).

"They shall never perish, neither shall any one pluck them out of my hand" (*John* x. 28).

"Fear not; I am the first and the last: I am he that liveth, and was dead; and, behold, I am alive for evermore, Amen; and have the keys of hell and of death" (*Rev.* i. 17, 18).

4. CHRIST'S LOVE.

Christ loveth with a love which passeth knowledge. He loved us as sinners; he loves us as his own, his chosen ones, his sheep, his friends, his bride. We need his love as truly as we need his strength. He loveth us individually; he loves us as members of that great multitude of the redeemed from among men, given him by the Father,—that church which belongs to him in so peculiar a way, and by so close a tie of relationship.

" For the husband is the head of the wife, even as Christ is the head of the church: and he is the saviour of the body. Therefore as the church is subject unto Christ, so let the wives be to their own husbands in every thing. Husbands, love your wives, even as Christ also loved the church, and gave himself for it; that he might sanctify and cleanse it with the washing of water by the word; that he might present it to himself a glorious church, not having spot, or wrinkle, or any such thing; but that it should be holy and without blemish " (*Eph.* v. 23–27).

" Let him kiss me with the kisses of his mouth: for thy love is better than wine. Because of the savour of thy good ointments thy name is as ointment poured forth, therefore do the virgins love thee. Draw me, we will run after thee: the king hath brought me into his chambers: we will be glad and rejoice in thee, we will remember thy love more than wine: the upright love thee" (*Cant.* i. 2–4).

"I am the rose of Sharon, and the lily of the valleys. As the lily among thorns, so is my love among the daughters. As the apple tree among the trees of the wood, so is my beloved among the sons. I sat down under his shadow with great delight, and his fruit was sweet to my taste. He brought me to the banqueting house, and his banner over me was love. Stay me with flagons, comfort me with apples: for I am sick of love. His left hand is under my head, and his right hand doth embrace me" (*Cant.* ii. 1–6).

"I am my beloved's, and his desire is toward me" (*Cant.* vii. 10).

5. CHRIST'S ADMIRATION.

There is more than love in Christ's feelings toward his church; there is admiration. As he said to Israel he says to her, "Thou wast perfect through the comeliness which I had put upon thee." The Song of Solomon is more full of *admiration* even than of *love*.

" Hearken, O daughter, and consider, and incline thine ear; forget also thine own people, and thy father's house; so shall the king greatly desire thy beauty: for he is thy Lord; and worship thou him. And the daughter of Tyre shall be there with a gift; even the rich among the people shall intreat thy favour. The king's daughter is all glorious within: her clothing is of wrought gold. She shall be brought unto the king in raiment of needlework: the virgins her companions that follow her shall be brought unto thee. With gladness and rejoicing shall they be brought: they shall enter into the king's palace" (*Ps.* xlv. 10–15).

" My beloved spake, and said unto me, Rise up, my love, my fair one, and come away. For, lo, the winter is past, the rain is over and gone; the flowers appear on the earth; the time of the singing of birds is come, and the voice of the turtle is heard in our land; the fig tree putteth forth her green figs, and the vines with the tender grape give a good smell. Arise, my love, my fair one, and come away. O my dove, that art in the clefts of the rock, in the secret places of the stairs, let me see thy countenance, let me hear thy voice; for sweet is thy voice, and thy countenance is comely" (*Cant.* ii. 10–14).

" Behold, thou art fair, my love; behold, thou art fair; thou hast doves' eyes within thy locks: thy hair is as a flock of goats, that appear from mount Gilead. Thy teeth are like a flock of sheep that are even shorn, which came up from the washing; whereof every one bear twins, and none is barren among them. Thy lips are like a thread of scarlet, and thy speech is comely: thy temples are like a piece of a pomegranate within thy locks. Thy neck is like the tower of David builded for an armoury, whereon there hang a thousand bucklers, all shields of mighty men. Thy two breasts are like two young roes that are twins, which feed among the lilies. Until the day break, and the shadows flee away, I will get me to the mountain of myrrh, and to the hill of frankincense. Thou art all fair, my love; there is no spot in thee. Come with me from Lebanon, my spouse, with me from Lebanon: look from the top of Amana, from the top of Shenir and Hermon, from the lions' dens, from the mountains of the leopards. Thou hast ravished my heart, my sister, my spouse; thou hast ravished my heart with one of thine eyes, with one chain of thy neck. How fair is thy love, my sister, my spouse! how much better is thy love than wine! and the smell of thine ointments than all spices! Thy lips, O my spouse, drop as the honeycomb: honey and milk are under thy tongue; and the smell of thy garments is like the smell of Lebanon " (*Cant.* iv. 1–11).

6. OF PERFECTION.

There is imperfection now, there will be perfection hereafter. Each one shall be perfect, soul and body; and the whole shall be perfect also; no flaw, no stain, no weakness, no possibility of failure or decay. The church is the perfection of creaturehood.

" That we all come unto a perfect man " (*Eph.* iv. 13).

" Ye are complete in him " (*Col.* ii. 10).

" To her was granted that she should be arrayed in fine linen, clean and white: for the fine linen is the righteousness of saints " (*Rev.* xix. 8).

" I John saw the holy city, new Jerusalem, coming down from God out of heaven, prepared as a bride adorned for her husband" (*Rev.* xxi. 2).

" A glorious church, not having spot, or wrinkle, or any such thing; but that it should be holy and without blemish " (*Eph.* v. 27).

" To present you holy and unblameable and unreproveable in his sight" (*Col.* i. 22).

" To him that is able to keep you from falling, and to present you faultless before the presence of his glory with exceeding joy, to the only wise God our Saviour, be glory and majesty, dominion and power, both now and ever. Amen " (*Jude* 24, 25).

7. OF UNITY.

" One Lord, one faith, one baptism, one God and Father of all ;" this is the church's watchword. Unity is hers, even now; for all her members are gathered round the one centre of the cross. But the day of complete unity is yet to come. She has this in promise and in hope.

" That they all may be one; as thou, Father, art in me, and I in thee, that they also may be one in us" (*John* xvii. 21).

" There shall be one fold, and one shepherd" (*John* x. 16).

" We, being many, are one body in Christ, and every one members one of another" (*Rom.* xii. 5).

" Ye are all one in Christ Jesus" (*Gal.* iii. 28).

" There is one body, and one Spirit, even as ye are called in one hope of your calling" (*Eph.* iv. 4).

" That they may be one, even as we are one: I in them, and thou in me, that they may be made perfect in one" (*John* xvii. 22, 23).

" We being many are one bread, and one body: for we are all partakers of that one bread" (1 *Cor.* x. 17).

" Till we all come in the unity of the faith, and of the knowledge of the Son of God, unto a perfect man, unto the measure of the stature of the fulness of Christ" (*Eph.* iv. 13).

" By one Spirit are we all baptized into one body, and have been all made to drink into one Spirit" (1 *Cor.* xii. 13).

" My dove, my undefiled is but one; she is the only one of her mother, she is the choice one of her that bare her" (*Cant.* vi. 9).

8. OF BEAUTY.

The church is the "beautiful flock" (Jer. xiii. 20), of which Israel was but the type. Christ not only washes her from her filthiness, but he makes her comely; he clothes her with beauty, his own beauty. There is beauty for her here; there is the promise of far greater and nobler beauty for her hereafter, when he comes to be "glorified IN his saints."

" Let me see thy countenance, let me hear thy voice; for sweet is thy voice, and thy countenance is comely" (*Cant.* ii. 14).

"Behold, thou art fair, my love; behold, thou art fair" (*Cant.* iv. 1).

"Thou art all fair, my love; there is no spot in thee" (*Cant.* iv. 7).

"O thou fairest among women" (*Cant.* v. 9).

"Thou art beautiful, O my love, as Tirzah, comely as Jerusalem" (*Cant.* vi. 4).

"Lo, a great multitude, which no man could number, of all nations, and kindreds, and people, and tongues, stood before the throne, and before the Lamb, clothed with white robes, and palms in their hands" (*Rev.* vii. 9).

"They have washed their robes, and made them white in the blood of the Lamb" (*Rev.* vii. 14).

9. OF HOLINESS.

"Holy and without blame before him in love" is the characteristic of the saint; and still more is such the characteristic of the church as a whole. She is the church "without spot;" all fair and holy, like him to whom she belongs.

" And to her (the Lamb's wife) was granted, that she should be arrayed in fine linen, clean and white: for the fine linen is the righteousness of saints " (*Rev.* xix. 8).

" After this I beheld, and, lo, a great multitude, which no man could number, of all nations, and kindreds, and people, and tongues, stood before the throne, and before the Lamb, clothed with white robes, and palms in their hands; and cried with a loud voice, saying, Salvation to our God which sitteth upon the throne, and unto the Lamb. And all the angels stood round about the throne, and about the elders and the four beasts, and fell before the throne on their faces, and worshipped God, saying, Amen: Blessing, and glory, and wisdom, and thanksgiving, and honour, and power, and might, be unto our God for ever and ever. Amen. And one of the elders answered, saying unto me, What are these which are arrayed in white robes? and whence came they? And I said unto him, Sir, thou knowest. And he said to me, These are they which came out of great tribulation, and have washed their robes, and made them white in the blood of the Lamb" (*Rev.* vii. 9–14).

"And he is the head of the body, the church: who is the beginning, the first-born from the dead; that in all things he might have the pre-eminence. For it pleased the Father that in him should all fulness dwell; and, having made peace through the blood of his cross, by him to reconcile all things unto himself; by him, I say, whether they be things in earth, or things in heaven. And you, that were sometime alienated, and enemies in your mind by wicked works, yet now hath he reconciled in the body of his flesh through death, to present you holy, and unblameable, and un-reproveable in his sight" (*Col.* i. 18–22).

10. OF THE SPIRIT AND HIS GIFTS.

The church is Christ's body, as it is written, "Ye are the body of Christ, and members in particular" (1 Cor. xii. 27); that is, ye as a whole form the body, and each of you is an individual member. From Christ, the Head, to whom has been given the Spirit without measure, flows down the Spirit to each member, and organ, and part of the body. The church has the Spirit only as belonging to Christ; she does not possess the Spirit by herself, but in and by her Head, apart from whom she is and has nothing. Of this Spirit she has the promise in virtue of her connection with Christ,—not with apostles or fathers, but with Christ himself. "It is like the precious ointment upon the head, that ran down upon the beard, even Aaron's beard, that went down to the skirts of his garments" (Ps. cxxxiii. 2).

"And in the midst of the seven candlesticks one like unto the Son of man, clothed with a garment down to the foot, and girt about the paps with a golden girdle. His head and his hairs where white like wool, as white as snow; and his eyes were as a flame of fire; and his feet like unto fine brass, as if they burned in a furnace; and his voice as the sound of many waters. and he had in his right hand seven stars: and out of his mouth went a sharp two-edged sword: and his countenance was as the sun shineth in his strength" (*Rev.* i. 13–16).

" But unto every one of us is given grace according to the measure of the gift of Christ. Wherefore he saith, When he ascended up on high, he led captivity captive, and gave gifts unto men. (Now that he ascended, what is it but that he also descended first into the lower parts of the earth? He that descended is the same also that ascended up far above all heavens, that he might fill all things.) And he gave some, apostles; and some, prophets; and some, evangelists; and some, pastors and teachers; for the perfecting of the saints, for the work of the ministry, for the edifying of the body of Christ: till we all come in the unity of the faith, and of the knowledge of the Son of God, unto a perfect man, unto the measure of the stature of the fulness of Christ " (*Eph.* iv. 7–13).

" And out of the throne proceeded lightnings and thunderings and voices: and there were seven lamps of fire burning before the throne, which are the seven Spirits of God " (*Rev.* iv. 5).

" And unto the angel of the church in Sardis write; These things saith he that hath the seven Spirits of God, and the seven stars; I know thy works, that thou hast a name that thou livest, and art dead " (*Rev.* iii. 1).

" Unto the angel of the church of Ephesus write; These things saith he that holdeth the seven stars in his right hand, who walketh in the midst of the seven golden candlesticks " (*Rev.* ii. 1).

" Even so ye, forasmuch as ye are zealous of spiritual gifts, seek that ye may excel to the edifying of the church. Wherefore let him that speaketh in an unknown tongue pray that he may interpret. For if I pray in an unknown tongue, my spirit prayeth, but my understanding is unfruitful. What is it then? I will pray with the spirit, and I will pray with the understanding also: I will sing with the spirit, and I will sing with the understanding also. Else, when thou shalt bless with the spirit, how shall he that occupieth the room of the unlearned say Amen at thy giving of thanks, seeing he understandeth not what thou sayest? For thou verily givest thanks well, but the other is not edified. I thank my God, I speak with tongues more than ye all: yet in the church I had rather speak five words with my understanding, that by my voice I might teach others also, than ten thousand words in an unknown tongue" (1 *Cor.* xiv. 12–19).

"Now there are diversities of gifts, but the same Spirit. And there are differences of administrations, but the same Lord. And there are diversities of operations, but it is the same God which worketh all in all. But the manifestation of the Spirit is given to every man to profit withal. For to one is given by the Spirit the word of wisdom; to another the word of knowledge by the same Spirit; to another faith by the same Spirit; to another the gifts of healing by the same Spirit; to another the working of miracles; to another prophecy; to another discerning of spirits; to another divers kinds of tongues; to another the interpretation of tongues: but all these worketh that one and the selfsame Spirit, dividing to every man severally as he will. For as the body is one, and hath many members, and all the members of that one body, being many, are one body : so also is Christ. For by one Spirit are we all baptized into one body, whether we be Jews or Gentiles, whether we be bond or free; and have been all made to drink into one Spirit " (1 *Cor.* xii. 4–13).

" And God hath set some in the church, first apostles, secondarily prophets, thirdly teachers, after that miracles, then gifts of healings, helps, governments, diversities of tongues. Are all apostles ? are all prophets ? are all teachers ? are all workers of miracles ? have all the gifts of healing ? do all speak with tongues ? do all interpret ? But covet earnestly the best gifts : and yet show I unto you a more excellent way " (1 *Cor.* xii. 28–31).

" For the body is not one member, but many. If the foot shall say, Because I am not the hand, I am not of the body; is it therefore not of the body ? and if the ear shall say, Because I am not the eye, I am

not of the body; is it therefore not of the
body? If the whole body were an eye,
where were the hearing? If the whole were
hearing, where were the smelling? But
now hath God set the members every one
of them in the body, as it hath pleased
him. And if they were all one member,
where were the body? But now are they
many members, yet but one body. And
the eye cannot say unto the hand, I have
no need of thee: nor again the head to the
feet, I have no need of you. Nay, much
more those members of the body, which
seem to be more feeble, are necessary: and
those members of the body, which we
think to be less honourable, upon these we
bestow more abundant honour; and our un-
comely parts have more abundant comeliness. For our comely parts have no need:
but God hath tempered the body together,
having given more abundant honour to
that part which lacked: that there should be
no schism in the body; but that the
members should have the same care one for
another. And whether one member suffer,
all the members suffer with it; or one

member be honoured, all the members rejoice with it. Now ye are the body of Christ, and members in particular" (1 *Cor.* xii. 14–27).

"I beheld; and, lo, in the midst of the throne and of the four beasts (living ones), and in the midst of the elders, stood a Lamb as it had been slain, having seven horns and seven eyes, which are the seven Spirits of God sent forth into all the earth" (*Rev.* v. 6).

11. OF GROWTH.

Individuals grow; the church grows. The church grows by additions from without; it grows also from within by fruitfulness, and holy expansion in all things that constitute her the church, in all the features of the Divine character. It grows as the olive, as the vine, as the body.

"From whom the whole body fitly joined together and compacted by that which every joint supplieth, according to the effectual working in the measure of every part, maketh increase of the body unto the edifying of itself in love" (*Eph*. iv. 16).

"Awake, O north wind; and come thou south; blow upon my garden, that the spices thereof may flow out. Let my beloved come into his garden, and eat his pleasant fruits" (*Cant*. iv. 16).

"Rooted and built up in him, and stablished in the faith, as ye have been taught, abounding therein with thanksgiving" (*Col*. ii. 7).

"The Head, from which all the body by joints and bands having nourishment ministered, and knit together, increaseth with the increase of God" (*Col*. ii. 19).

"May grow up into him in all things" (*Eph*. iv. 15).

12. OF FRUITFULNESS.

"Be fruitful" is a word for the church, fruitful in all things. Not dry and withered in stem, or branch, or leaf; but green, ever green; fruitful, ever fruitful; flourishing like the palm-tree and the cedar.

" Herein is my Father glorified, that ye bear much fruit" (*John* xv. 8).

" Let us get up early to the vineyards; let us see if the vine flourish, whether the tender grape appear, and the pomegranates bud forth" (*Cant.* vii. 12).

" He purgeth it, that it may bring forth more fruit" (*John* xv. 2).

" Thy mother is like a vine in thy blood, planted by the waters: she was fruitful and full of branches by reason of many waters. And she had strong rods for the sceptres of them that bare rule, and her stature was exalted among the thick branches, and she appeared in her height with the multitude of her branches" (*Ezek.* xix. 10, 11).*

13. Of Final Conquest.

The church seems for the present upon the losing side. She is the injured widow; she is the little flock. She does not triumph now, and often has she been trodden down. But she is one day to overcome, to receive a kingdom;

* Though this passage refers specially to Israel, it symbolizes the church's fruitfulness as well.

and instead of shame, poverty, death, perse-
cution, to obtain glory, and riches, and life,
and endless victory.

" And the seventh angel sounded; and
there were great voices in heaven, saying,
The kingdoms of this world are become
the kingdoms of our Lord, and of his Christ;
and he shall reign for ever and ever. And
the four and twenty elders, which sat before
God on their seats, fell upon their faces, and
worshipped God, saying, We give thee thanks,
O Lord God Almighty, which art, and wast,
and art to come; because thou hast taken to
thee thy great power, and hast reigned. And
the nations were angry, and thy wrath is
come, and the time of the dead, that they
should be judged, and that thou shouldest
give reward unto thy servants the prophets,
and to the saints, and them that fear thy
name, small and great; and shouldest destroy
them which destroy the earth " (*Rev.* xi.
15–18).

" Whose voice then shook the earth: but
now he hath promised, saying, Yet once
more I shake not the earth only, but also

heaven. And this word, Yet once more, signifieth the removing of those things that are shaken, as of things that are made, that those things which cannot be shaken may remain. Wherefore we receiving a kingdom which cannot be moved, let us have grace, whereby we may serve God acceptably with reverence and godly fear" (*Heb.* xii. 26–28).

"And he that overcometh, and keepeth my works unto the end, to him will I give power over the nations: and he shall rule them with a rod of iron; as the vessels of a potter shall they be broken to shivers: even as I received of my Father. And I will give him the morning star" (*Rev.* ii. 26–28).

"And they cried with a loud voice, saying, How long, O Lord, holy and true, dost thou not judge and avenge our blood on them that dwell on the earth? And white robes were given unto every one of them; and it was said unto them, that they should rest yet for a little season, until their fellow-servants also and their brethren, that should

be killed as they were, should be fulfilled "
(*Rev.* vi. 10, 11).

"All the ends of the world shall remember
and turn unto the Lord: and all the kindreds of the nations shall worship before
thee.   For the kingdom is the Lord's:
and he is the governor among the nations"
(*Ps.* xxii. 27, 28).

"And I heard a loud voice saying in
heaven, Now is come salvation, and strength,
and the kingdom of our God, and the power
of his Christ: for the accuser of our brethren
is cast down, which accused them before our
God day and night.   And they overcame
him by the blood of the Lamb, and by the
word of their testimony ; and they loved
not their lives unto the death " (*Rev.* xii.
10, 11).

"And I saw heaven opened, and behold
a white horse ; and he that sat upon him
was called Faithful and True, and in
righteousness he doth judge and make war.
His eyes were as a flame of fire, and on his
head were many crowns ; and he had a name
written, that no man knew, but he himself.

And he was clothed with a vesture dipped in blood : and his name is called The Word of God. And the armies which were in heaven followed him upon white horses, clothed in fine linen, white and clean. And out of his mouth goeth a sharp sword, that with it he should smite the nations : and he shall rule them with a rod of iron : and he treadeth the winepress of the fierceness and wrath of Almighty God. And he hath on his vesture and on his thigh a name written, KING OF KINGS, AND LORD OF LORDS" (*Rev.* xix. 11–16).

"And the kingdom and dominion, and the greatness of the kingdom under the whole heaven, shall be given to the people of the saints of the most High, whose kingdom is an everlasting kingdom, and all dominions shall serve and obey him" (*Dan.* vii. 27).

14. OF GLORY.

It doth not yet appear what she shall be. She is clothed with poor raiment here, for this is not her rest nor her home ; but her glory is coming, and she shall shine like the sun. After the present shame there comes the everlasting glory.

" The king's daughter is all glorious within : her clothing is of wrought gold. She shall be brought unto the king in raiment of needlework : the virgins her companions that follow her shall be brought unto thee " (*Ps.* xlv. 13, 14).

" And I saw a new heaven and a new earth : for the first heaven and the first earth were passed away ; and there was no more sea. And I John saw the holy city, new Jerusalem, coming down from God out of heaven, prepared as a bride adorned for her husband. And I heard a great voice out of heaven, saying, Behold, the tabernacle of God is with men, and he will dwell with them, and they shall be his people, and God himself shall be with them, and be their God. And God shall wipe away all tears from their eyes ; and there shall be no more death, neither sorrow, nor crying, neither shall there be any more pain : for the former things are passed away. And he that sat upon the throne said, Behold, I make all things new. And he said unto me, Write: for these words are true and faithful" (*Rev.* xxi. 1–5).

" That he might present it to himself **a** glorious church " (*Eph.* v. 27).

" When he shall come to be glorified in his saints, and to be admired in all them that believe " (2 *Thess.* i. 10).

" That ye would walk worthy of God, who hath called you unto his kingdom and glory " (1 *Thess.* ii. 12).

" And there came unto me one of the seven angels which had the seven vials full of the seven last plagues, and talked with me, saying, Come hither, I will show thee the bride, the Lamb's wife. And he carried me away in the spirit to a great and high mountain, and showed me that great city, the holy Jerusalem, descending out of heaven from God, having the glory of God: and her light was like unto a stone most precious, even like a jasper stone, clear as crystal ; and had a wall great and high, and had twelve gates, and at |the gates twelve angels, and names written thereon, which are the names of the twelve tribes of the children of Israel: on the east three gates; on the north three gates; on the south three gates; and on the west three gates. And the wall of the city had twelve foundations, and in them the names of the twelve apostles of the Lamb. And he that talked with me had a golden reed to measure the city, and the gates thereof, and the wall thereof. And the city lieth four-square, and the length is as large as the breadth: and he measured the city with the reed, twelve thousand furlongs. The length and the breadth and the height of it are equal. And he measured the wall thereof, an hundred and forty and four cubits, according to the measure of a man, that is, of the angel. And the building of the wall of it was of jasper: and the city was pure gold, like unto clear glass. And the foundations of the wall of the city were garnished with all manner of precious stones. The first foundation was jasper; the second, sapphire; the third, a chalcedony; the fourth, an emerald; the fifth, sardonyx; the sixth, sardius; the seventh, chrysolyte; the eighth, beryl; the ninth, a topaz; the tenth, a chrysoprasus; the eleventh, a jacinth; the twelfth, an amethyst. And the twelve gates were twelve pearls; every several gate was of one pearl: and the street of the city was pure gold, as it were transparent glass. And I saw no temple therein: for the Lord God Almighty and the Lamb are the temple of it. And the city had no need of the sun, neither of the moon, to shine in it, for the glory of God did lighten it, and the Lamb is the light thereof. And the nations of them which are saved shall walk in the light of it: and the kings of the earth do bring their glory and honour into it. And the gates of it shall not be shut at all by day: for there shall be no night there. And they shall bring the glory and honour of the nations into it " (*Rev.* xxi. 9-26).

CHAPTER IV.

FOR ISRAEL.

A VERY large portion of Scripture has been written for Israel, and has to do with Israel's history. The past, present, and future of that nation are brought before us at great length; God thus teaching us the prominence which it has in his purposes, and the importance of the place which it occupies in the world, both for good and for evil. Why God should have connected so much of the story of past ages with Israel, and why that name occurs so often in the inspired visions of future ages, is not for us to say. " O the depth of the riches both of the wisdom and knowledge of God! how unsearchable are his judgments, and his ways past finding out!"

That Israel's marvellous past and future are not merely for the glory of the nation, nor yet merely for blessing to the world, but for the glory of the name of the Lord God of Israel, for the manifestation of Jehovah himself, we know; and yet if any one truth or lesson more than another be deducible from all that has been recorded and foretold of that nation, it is the blessed message contained in that text, "Where sin abounded, grace did much more abound." Christ's gospel finds its amplest and brightest illustration in Israel's history,— a history of sin to the uttermost, and salvation to the uttermost.

Our business is not to expound nor to illustrate that history, but simply to arrange the predictions of the prophets regarding it, leaving our readers to interpret for themselves.

Nor shall we attempt to give at full length all the prophecies regarding Israel's future. Were we to do so we might transcribe nearly the whole of the prophets, greater and smaller. Our selections must be brief and limited, little more than specimens ; yet they may furnish heads under which our readers can, at their leisure, gather and arrange the future story of the nation "meted out and trodden down," "scattered, spoiled," yet still "beloved for their fathers' sakes."

To Israel belonged "the promises" of old (Rom. ix. 4); the great treasure-house of promise was entrusted to their keeping, that they might keep it unrifled, and hand it onward age after age, till He should come to whom the promise was made. The first promise given in Paradise, and all subsequent ones, were gathered together and committed to Israel, through them to be communicated to the world in the fulness of time.

In like manner Israel is herself the subject of promises. They cluster round her like unearthly gems, adorning—we might almost say mocking—the sackcloth in which she now sits, and has sat for ages.

In these promises we can read blessing to the church, for they illustrate God's character, and unfold his purposes of grace. But still, though we can gather much out of them for consolation, for hope, for joy, for holiness, we must not rob Israel of her heritage, nor forget that she, on whom the curses have fallen so long and heavily, is the same to whom marvellous blessing has been promised.

1. REPENTANCE.

"They shall come with weeping, and with supplications will I lead them : I will cause them to walk by the rivers of waters in a straight way, wherein they shall not stumble : for I am a father to Israel, and Ephraim is my firstborn" (*Jer.* xxxi. 9).

" And there is hope in thine end, saith the Lord, that thy children shall come again to their own border. I have surely heard Ephraim bemoaning himself thus ; Thou hast chastised me, and I was chastised, as a bullock unaccustomed to the yoke: turn thou me, and I shall be turned ; for thou art the Lord my God. Surely after that I was turned, I repented ; and after that I was instructed, I smote upon my thigh : I was ashamed, yea, even confounded, because I did bear the reproach of my youth. Is Ephraim my dear son ? is he a pleasant child ? for since I spake against him, I do earnestly remember him still ; therefore my bowels are troubled for him ; I will surely have mercy upon him, saith the Lord. Set thee up waymarks, make thee high heaps : set thine heart toward the highway, even the way which thou wentest : turn again, O virgin of Israel, turn again to these thy cities " (*Jer*. xxxi. 17–21).

" And I will pour upon the house of David, and upon the inhabitants of Jerusalem, the spirit of grace and of supplications:

and they shall look upon me whom they have pierced, and they shall mourn for him, as one mourneth for his only son, and shall be in bitterness for him, as one that is in bitterness for his firstborn " (*Zech.* xii. 10).

" Nevertheless I will remember my covenant with thee in the days of thy youth, and I will establish unto thee an everlasting covenant. Then thou shalt remember thy ways, and be ashamed, when thou shalt receive thy sisters, thine elder and thy younger: and I will give them unto thee for daughters, but not by thy covenant. And I will establish my covenant with thee; and thou shalt know that I am the Lord: that thou mayest remember, and be confounded, and never open thy mouth any more because of thy shame, when I am pacified toward thee for all that thou hast done, saith the Lord God" (*Ezek.* xvi. 60–63).

" In those days, and in that time, saith the Lord, the children of Israel shall come, they and the children of Judah together, going and weeping: they shall go, and seek the Lord their God. They shall ask the way to Zion with their faces thitherward, saying, Come, and let us join ourselves to the Lord in a perpetual covenant that shall not be forgotten " (*Jer.* l. 4, 5).

"And I will give them an heart to know me, that I am the Lord : and they shall be my people, and I will be their God : for they shall return unto me with their whole heart" (*Jer.* xxiv. 7).

2. CONSOLATION.

" Thus saith the Lord ; A voice was heard in Ramah, lamentation, and bitter weeping ; Rahel weeping for her children refused to be comforted for her children, because they were not. Thus saith the Lord ; Refrain thy voice from weeping, and thine eyes from tears : for thy work shall be rewarded, saith the Lord ; and they shall come again from the land of the enemy " (*Jer.* xxxi. 15, 16).

" As one whom his mother comforteth, so will I comfort you ; and ye shall be comforted in Jerusalem. And when ye see this, your heart shall rejoice, and your bones shall flourish like an herb : and the hand of the Lord shall be known toward his servants, and his indignation toward his enemies " (*Isa.* lxvi. 13, 14).

" Fear thou not ; for I am with thee : be not dismayed ; for I am thy God : I will strengthen thee ; yea, I will help thee ; yea, I will uphold thee with the right hand of my righteousness. Behold, all they that were incensed against thee shall be ashamed and confounded : they shall be as nothing ; and they that strive with thee shall perish. Thou shalt seek them, and shalt not find them, even them that contended with thee : they that war against thee shall be as nothing, and as a thing of nought. For I the Lord thy God will hold thy right hand, saying unto thee, Fear not ; I will help thee. Fear not, thou worm Jacob, and ye men of Israel ; I will help thee, saith the Lord, and thy redeemer, the Holy One of Israel " (*Isa.* xli. 10–14).

" And therefore will the Lord wait, that he may be gracious unto you, and therefore will he be exalted, that he may have mercy upon you: for the Lord is a God of judgment: blessed are all they that wait for him. For the people shall dwell in Zion at Jerusalem: thou shalt weep no more: he will be very gracious unto thee at the voice of thy cry; when he shall hear it, he will answer thee. And though the Lord give you the bread of adversity, and the water of affliction, yet shall not thy teachers be removed into a corner any more, but thine eyes shall see thy teachers" (*Isa.* xxx. 18–20).

"Sing, O barren, thou that didst not bear; break forth into singing, and cry aloud, thou that didst not travail with child: for more are the children of the desolate than the children of the married wife, saith the Lord. Enlarge the place of thy tent, and let them stretch forth the curtains of thine habitations: spare not, lengthen thy cords, and strengthen thy stakes; for thou shalt break forth on the right hand and on the left; and thy seed shall inherit the Gentiles, and make the desolate cities to be inhabited. Fear not;

for thou shalt not be ashamed: neither be
thou confounded; for thou shalt not be put
to shame: for thou shalt forget the shame of
thy youth, and shalt not remember the
reproach of thy widowhood any more.
For thy Maker is thine husband; the Lord
of hosts is his name; and thy Redeemer
the Holy One of Israel; the God of the
whole earth shall he be called. For the
Lord hath called thee as a woman forsaken
and grieved in spirit, and a wife of youth,
when thou wast refused, saith thy God.
For a small moment have I forsaken thee;
but with great mercies will I gather thee.
In a little wrath I hid my face from
thee for a moment; but with everlasting
kindness will I have mercy on thee, saith
the Lord thy Redeemer. For this is as
the waters of Noah unto me: for as I have
sworn that the waters of Noah should no
more go over the earth; so have I sworn
that I would not be wroth with thee, nor
rebuke thee. For the mountains shall
depart, and the hills be removed; but my
kindness shall not depart from thee, neither
shall the covenant of my peace be removed,

saith the Lord that hath mercy on thee"
(*Isa.* liv. 1–10).

3. FORGIVENESS.

" Remember these, O Jacob and Israel;
for thou art my servant: I have formed
thee; thou art my servant: O Israel, thou
shalt not be forgotten of me. I have blotted
out, as a thick cloud, thy transgressions,
and, as a cloud, thy sins: return unto me;
for I have redeemed thee. Sing, O ye
heavens; for the Lord hath done it: shout,
ye lower parts of the earth: break forth
into singing, ye mountains, O forest, and
every tree therein: for the Lord hath redeemed Jacob, and glorified himself in
Israel " (*Isa.* xliv. 21–23).

" In that day there shall be a fountain
opened to the house of David and to the
inhabitants of Jerusalem for sin and for
uncleanness" (*Zech.* xiii. 1).

" Then will I sprinkle clean water upon
you, and ye shall be clean: from all your
filthiness, and from all your idols, will I

cleanse you.   A new heart also will I give
you, and a new spirit will I put within you:
and I will take away the stony heart out of
your flesh, and I will give you an heart of
flesh.   And I will put my Spirit within
you, and cause you to walk in my statutes,
and ye shall keep my judgments, and do
them.   And ye shall dwell in the land that
I gave to your fathers; and ye shall be my
people, and I will be your God.   I will also
save you from all your uncleannesses; and
I will call for the corn, and will increase it,
and lay no famine upon you.   And I will
multiply the fruit of the tree, and the increase of the field, that ye shall receive no
more reproach of famine among the heathen.
Then shall ye remember your own evil
ways, and your doings that were not good,
and shall loathe yourselves in your own
sight for your iniquities and for your abo-
minations" (*Ezek.* xxxvi. 25–31).

4. THE HOLY SPIRIT.

" And the Redeemer shall come to Zion,
and unto them that turn from transgres-

sion in Jacob, saith the Lord. As for me,
this is my covenant with them, saith the
Lord; My Spirit that is upon thee, and my
words which I have put in thy mouth,
shall not depart out of thy mouth, nor out
of the mouth of thy seed, nor out of the
mouth of thy seed's seed, saith the Lord,
from henceforth and for ever" (*Isa.* lix.
20, 21).

" Until the Spirit be poured upon us
from on high, and the wilderness be a fruitful field, and the fruitful field be counted
for a forest. Then judgment shall dwell in
the wilderness, and righteousness remain in
the fruitful field" (*Isa.* xxxii. 15).

" Thus saith the Lord that made thee, and
formed thee from the womb, which will help
thee; Fear not, O Jacob, my servant; and
thou, Jesurun, whom I have chosen. For I
will pour water upon him that is thirsty, and
floods upon the dry ground: I will pour
my spirit upon thy seed, and my blessing
upon thine offspring" (*Isa.* xliv. 2, 3).

" O thou that art named the house of
Jacob, is the spirit of the Lord straitened?

are these his doings? do not my words do
good to him that walketh uprightly?" (*Micah*
ii. 7.)

5. JOY.

" Sing, O daughter of Zion; shout, O
Israel; be glad and rejoice with all the
heart, O daughter of Jerusalem. The Lord
hath taken away thy judgments, he hath
cast out thine enemy: the King of Israel,
even the Lord, is in the midst of thee: thou
shalt not see evil any more. In that day
it shall be said to Jerusalem, Fear thou
not: and to Zion, Let not thine hands be
slack. The Lord thy God in the midst
of thee is mighty; he will save, he will
rejoice over thee with joy; he will rest in
his love, he will joy over thee with singing.
I will gather them that are sorrowful for
the solemn assembly, who are of thee, to
whom the reproach of it was a burden
(*Zeph.* iii. 14–18).

" Behold, these shall come from far: and,
lo, these from the north and from the west;
and these from the land of Sinim. Sing, O

heavens; and be joyful, O earth; and break forth into singing, O mountains: for the Lord hath comforted his people, and will have mercy upon his afflicted. But Zion said, The Lord hath forsaken me, and my Lord hath forgotten me. Can a woman forget her sucking child, that she should not have compassion on the son of her womb? yea, they may forget, yet will I not forget thee. Behold, I have graven thee upon the palms of my hands; thy walls are continually before me. Thy children shall make haste; thy destroyers, and they that made thee waste, shall go forth of thee. Lift up thine eyes round about, and behold: all these gather themselves together, and come to thee. As I live, saith the Lord, thou shalt surely clothe thee with them all, as with an ornament, and bind them on thee, as a bride doeth" (*Isa.* xlix. 12–18).

" How beautiful upon the mountains are the feet of him that bringeth good tidings, that publisheth peace; that bringeth good tidings of good, that publisheth salvation; that saith unto Zion, Thy God reigneth!

Thy watchmen shall lift up the voice ; with the voice together shall they sing : for they shall see eye to eye, when the Lord shall bring again Zion " (*Isa.* lii. 7, 8).

" And in that day thou shalt say, O Lord, I will praise thee : though thou wast angry with me, thine anger is turned away, and thou comfortedst me. Behold, God is my salvation ; I will trust, and not be afraid : for the Lord JEHOVAH is my strength and my song ; he also is become my salvation. Therefore with joy shall ye draw water out of the wells of salvation " (*Isa.* xii. 1–3).

6. VICTORY OVER ENEMIES.

" For thou hast made of a city an heap ; of a defenced city a ruin : a palace of strangers to be no city ; it shall never be built. Therefore shall the strong people glorify thee, the city of the terrible nations shall fear thee. For thou hast been a strength to the poor, a strength to the needy in his distress, a refuge from the storm, a shadow from the heat, when the blast of the terrible ones is as a storm against the wall. Thou shalt bring down the noise of strangers as the heat in a dry place; even the heat with the shadow of a cloud: the branch of the terrible ones shall be brought low" (*Isa.* xxv. 2–5).

"Therefore saith the Lord, the Lord of hosts, the mighty One of Israel, Ah, I will ease me of mine adversaries, and avenge me of mine enemies. And I will turn my hand upon thee, and purely purge away thy dross, and take away all thy tin: and I will restore thy judges as at the first, and thy counsellors as at the beginning: afterward thou shalt be called, The city of righteousness, the faithful city. Zion shall be redeemed with judgment, and her converts with righteousness" (*Isa.* i. 24–27).

"Arise and thresh, O daughter of Zion: for I will make thine horn iron, and I will make thy hoofs brass: and thou shalt beat in pieces many people: and I will consecrate their gain unto the Lord, and their substance unto the Lord of the whole earth" (*Micah* iv. 13).

7. DELIVERANCE.

" Then shall the Lord go forth, and fight
against those nations, as when he fought in
the day of battle. And his feet shall stand
in that day upon the mount of Olives, which
is before Jerusalem on the east, and the
mount of Olives shall cleave in the midst
thereof toward the east and toward the west,
and there shall be a very great valley; and
half of the mountain shall remove toward the
north, and half of it toward the south. And
ye shall flee to the valley of the mountains;
for the valley of the mountains shall reach
unto Azal : yea, ye shall flee, like as ye fled
from before the earthquake in the days of
Uzziah king of Judah : and the Lord my
God shall come, and all the saints with thee.
And it shall come to pass in that day, that
the light shall not be clear, nor dark : but
it shall be one day which shall be known to
the Lord, not day, nor night : but it shall
come to pass, that at evening time it shall
be light. And it shall be in that day, that
living waters shall go out from Jerusalem;

half of them toward the former sea, and half of them toward the hinder sea : in summer and in winter shall it be. And the Lord shall be king over all the earth : in that day shall there be one Lord, and his name one " (*Zech.* xiv. 3–9).

" But I am the Lord thy God, that divided the sea, whose waves roared : The Lord of hosts is his name. And I have put my words in thy mouth, and I have covered thee with the shadow of mine hand, that I may plant the heavens, and lay the foundations of the earth, and say unto Zion, Thou art my people. Awake, awake, stand up, O Jerusalem, which hast drunk at the hand of the Lord the cup of his fury ; thou hast drunken the dregs of the cup of trembling, and wrung them out " (*Isa.* li. 15–17).

" Jerusalem shall be inhabited again in her own place, even in Jerusalem. The Lord also shall save the tents of Judah first, that the glory of the house of David and the glory of the inhabitants of Jerusalem do not magnify themselves against Judah. In that day shall the Lord defend the inhab-

itants of Jerusalem ; and he that is feeble
among them at that day shall be as David ;
and the house of David shall be as God, as
the angel of the Lord before them.　And
it shall come to pass in that day, that I will
seek to destroy all the nations that come
against Jerusalem " (*Zech.* xii. 6–9).

8. LIFE.

" Then he said unto me, Son of man,
these bones are the whole house of Israel :
behold, they say, Our bones are dried, and
our hope is lost : we are cut off for our
parts.　Therefore prophesy and say unto
them, Thus saith the Lord God ; Behold, O
my people, I will open your graves, and
cause you to come up out of your graves,
and bring you into the land of Israel.　And
ye shall know that I am the Lord, when I
have opened your graves, O my people, and
brought you up out of your graves, and
shall put my spirit in you, and ye shall
live, and I shall place you in your own
land : then shall ye know that I the Lord

have spoken it, and performed it, saith the Lord" (*Ezek.* xxxvii. 11–14).

"Therefore I will judge you, O house of Israel, every one according to his ways, saith the Lord God. Repent, and turn yourselves from all your transgressions ; so iniquity shall not be your ruin. Cast away from you all your transgressions, whereby ye have transgressed ; and make you a new heart and a new spirit : for why will ye die, O house of Israel ? For I have no pleasure in the death of him that dieth, saith the Lord God : wherefore turn yourselves, and live ye" (*Ezek.* xviii. 30–32).

"For thus saith the Lord unto the house of Israel, Seek ye me, and ye shall live : but seek not Beth-el, nor enter into Gilgal, and pass not to Beer-sheba : for Gilgal shall surely go into captivity, and Beth-el shall come to nought. Seek the Lord, and ye shall live ; lest he break out like fire in the house of Joseph, and devour it, and there be none to quench it in Beth-el. Ye who turn judgment to wormwood, and leave off righteousness in the earth, seek him that

maketh the seven stars and Orion, and
turneth the shadow of death into the morning, and maketh the day dark with night:
that calleth for the waters of the sea, and
poureth them out upon the face of the
earth : The Lord is his name. Seek good,
and not evil, that ye may live : and so the
Lord, the God of hosts, shall be with you,
as ye have spoken " (*Amos* v. 4–8, 14).

9. UNITY AND PEACE.

"Moreover, thou son of man, take thee
one stick, and write upon it, For Judah,
and for the children of Israel his companions: then take another stick, and write
upon it, For Joseph, the stick of Ephraim,
and for all the house of Israel his companions: and join them one to another into
one stick ; and they shall become one in
thine hand. And when the children of thy
people shall speak unto thee, saying, Wilt
thou not shew us what thou meanest by
these ? say unto them, Thus saith the
Lord God; Behold, I will take the stick of
Joseph, which is in the hand of Ephraim,

and the tribes of Israel his fellows, and will
put them with him, even with the stick of
Judah, and make them one stick, and they
shall be one in mine hand. And the sticks
whereon thou writest shall be in thine hand
before their eyes. And say unto them, Thus
saith the Lord God; Behold, I will take the
children of Israel from among the heathen,
whither they be gone, and will gather them
on every side, and bring them into their own
land: and I will make them one nation in
the land upon the mountains of Israel; and
one king shall be king to them all: and
they shall be no more two nations, neither
shall they be divided into two kingdoms
any more at all: neither shall they defile
themselves any more with their idols, nor
with their detestable things, nor with any
of their transgressions: but I will save them
out of all their dwelling-places, wherein they
have sinned, and will cleanse them: so shall
they be my people, and I will be their God.
And David my servant shall be king over
them; and they all shall have one shepherd: they shall also walk in my judgments,
and observe my statutes, and do them.

And they shall dwell in the land that I
have given unto Jacob my servant, wherein
your fathers have dwelt; and they shall
dwell therein, even they, and their children,
and their children's children for ever: and
my servant David shall be their prince for
ever.   Moreover I will make a covenant
of peace with them; it shall be an everlasting covenant with them: and I will
place them, and multiply them, and will set
my sanctuary in the midst of them for
evermore.   My tabernacle also shall be
with them: yea, I will be their God, and
they shall be my people" (*Ezek.* xxxvii.
16–27).

"With righteousness shall he judge the
poor, and reprove with equity for the meek
of the earth: and he shall smite the earth with
the rod of his mouth, and with the breath of
his lips shall he slay the wicked.   And righteousness shall be the girdle of his loins, and
faithfulness the girdle of his reins.   The wolf
also shall dwell with the lamb, and the leopard
shall lie down with the kid; and the calf and
the young lion and the fatling together; and

a little child shall lead them. And the cow and the bear shall feed; their young ones shall lie down together: and the lion shall eat straw like the ox. And the sucking child shall play on the hole of the asp, and the weaned child shall put his hand on the cockatrice' den. They shall not hurt nor destroy in all my holy mountain: for the earth shall be full of the knowledge of the Lord, as the waters cover the sea. (*Isa.* xi. 4–9).

" And it shall come to pass in the last days, that the mountain of the Lord's house shall be established in the top of the mountains, and shall be exalted above the hills; and all nations shall flow unto it. And many people shall go and say, Come ye, and let us go up to the mountain of the Lord, to the house of the God of Jacob; and he will teach us of his ways, and we will walk in his paths: for out of Zion shall go forth the law, and the word of the Lord from Jerusalem. And he shall judge among the nations, and shall rebuke many people: and they shall beat their swords into plough-

shares, and their spears into pruning-hooks :
nation shall not lift up sword against nation,
neither shall they learn war any more. O
house of Jacob, come ye, and let us walk in
the light of the Lord " (*Isa.* ii. 2–5).

10. HOLINESS.

" And he shall sit as a refiner and purifier
of silver: and he shall purify the sons of
Levi, and purge them as gold and silver,
that they may offer unto the Lord an
offering in righteousness. Then shall the
offering of Judah and Jerusalem be pleasant
unto the Lord, as in the days of old, and as
in former years " (*Mal.* iii. 3, 4).

" And it shall come to pass, that he that
is left in Zion, and he that remaineth in
Jerusalem, shall be called holy, even every
one that is written among the living in
Jerusalem: when the Lord shall have
washed away the filth of the daughters of
Zion, and shall have purged the blood of
Jerusalem from the midst thereof by the
spirit of judgment, and by the spirit of
burning " *Isa.* (iv. 3, 4).

"So shall ye know that I am the Lord your God dwelling in Zion, my holy mountain: then shall Jerusalem be holy, and there shall no strangers pass through her any more" (*Joel* iii. 17).

11. THE COVENANT.

"This shall be the covenant that I will make with the house of Israel; After those days, saith the Lord, I will put my law in their inward parts, and write it in their hearts; and will be their God, and they shall be my people. And they shall teach no more every man his neighbour, and every man his brother, saying, Know the Lord: for they shall all know me, from the least of them unto the greatest of them, saith the Lord: for I will forgive their iniquity, and I will remember their sin no more" (*Jer.* xxxi. 33, 34).

"In that day will I make a covenant for them with the beasts of the field, and with the fowls of heaven, and with the creeping things of the ground: and I will break the bow and the sword and the battle out of the earth, and will make them to lie down safely. And I will betroth thee unto me for ever; yea, I will betroth thee unto me in righteousness, and in judgmen, and in loving-kindness, and in mercies. I will even betroth thee unto me in faithfulness: and thou shalt know the Lord. And it shall come to pass in that day, I will hear, saith the Lord, I will hear the heavens, and they shall hear the earth; and the earth shall hear the corn, and the wine, and the oil; and they shall hear Jezreel. And I will sow her unto me in the earth; and I will have mercy upon her that had not obtained mercy; and I will say to them which were not my people, Thou art my people; and they shall say, Thou art my God" (*Hos.* ii. 18–23).

"For I the Lord love judgment, I hate robbery for burnt offering; and I will direct their work in truth, and I will make an everlasting covenant with them. And their seed shall be known among the Gentiles, and their offspring among the people: all that see them shall acknowledge them, that they are the seed which the Lord hath blessed" (*Isa.* lxi. 8, 9).

" Nevertheless I will remember my covenant with thee in the days of thy youth, and I will establish unto thee an everlasting covenant. Then thou shalt remember thy ways, and be ashamed, when thou shalt receive thy sisters, thine elder and thy younger : and I will give them unto thee for daughters, but not by thy covenant. And I will establish my covenant with thee ; and thou shalt know that I am the Lord : that thou mayest remember, and be confounded, and never open thy mouth any more because of thy shame, when I am pacified toward thee for all that thou hast done, saith the Lord God " (*Ezek.* xvi. 60–63).

12. Righteousness and Security.

" In those days, and at that time, will I cause the Branch of righteousness to grow up unto David ; and he shall execute judgment and righteousness in the land. In those days shall Judah be saved, and Jerusalem shall dwell safely : and this is the name wherewith she shall be called, The Lord our righteousness " (*Jer.* xxxiii. 15, 16).

" Behold, the days come, saith the Lord, that I will raise unto David a righteous Branch, and a King shall reign and prosper, and shall execute judgment and justice in the earth. In his days Judah shall be saved, and Israel shall dwell safely : and this is his name whereby he shall be called, THE LORD OUR RIGHTEOUSNESS " (*Jer.* xxiii. 5, 6).

" The Lord is exalted ; for he dwelleth on high : he hath filled Zion with judgment and righteousness. And wisdom and knowledge shall be the stability of thy times, and strength of salvation : the fear of the Lord is his treasure " (*Isa.* xxxiii. 5, 6).

" In that day shall this song be sung in the land of Judah ; We have a strong city ; salvation will God appoint for walls and bulwarks. Open ye the gates, that the righteous nation which keepeth the truth may enter in. Thou wilt keep him in

perfect peace, whose mind is stayed on thee :
because he trusteth in thee. Trust ye in the
Lord for ever : for in the Lord JEHOVAH
is everlasting strength " (*Isa.* xxvi. 1–4).

" In righteousness shalt thou be established : thou shalt be far from oppression ;
for thou shalt not fear : and from terror ;
for it shall not come near thee. Behold,
they shall surely gather together, but not by
me : whosoever shall gather together against
thee shall fall for thy sake. Behold, I have
created the smith that bloweth the coals in
the fire, and that bringeth forth an instrument
for his work ; and I have created the waster
to destroy. No weapon that is formed
against thee shall prosper ; and every tongue
that shall rise against thee in judgment thou
shalt condemn. This is the heritage of the
servants of the Lord, and their righteousness is of me, saith the Lord " (*Isa.* liv.
14–17).

13. LOVE.

" I will mention the loving-kindnesses
of the Lord, and the praises of the Lord,

according to all that the Lord hath bestowed on us, and the great goodness toward the house of Israel, which he hath bestowed on them according to his mercies, and according to the multitude of his loving-kindnesses. For he said, Surely they are my people, children that will not lie: so he was their Saviour. In all their affliction he was afflicted, and the angel of his presence saved them: in his love and in his pity he redeemed them; and he bare them, and carried them all the days of old " (*Isa.* lxiii. 7–9).

" Therefore, behold, I will allure her, and bring her into the wilderness, and speak comfortably unto her. And I will give her vineyards from thence, and the valley of Achor for a door of hope: and she shall sing there, as in the days of her youth, and as in the day when she came up out of the land of Egypt " (*Hos.* ii. 14, 15).

" I will heal their backsliding, I will love them freely: for mine anger is turned away from him. I will be as the dew unto Israel: he shall grow as the lily, and cast forth his roots as Lebanon. His branches shall spread, and his beauty shall be as the olive tree, and his smell as Lebanon. They that dwell under his shadow shall return; they shall revive as the corn, and grow as the vine: the scent thereof shall be as the wine of Lebanon" (*Hos.* xiv. 4–7).

14. HONOUR.

"And strangers shall stand and feed your flocks, and the sons of the alien shall be your plowmen and your vine-dressers. But ye shall be named the Priests of the Lord: men shall call you the Ministers of our God: ye shall eat the riches of the Gentiles, and in their glory shall ye boast yourselves" (*Isa.* lxi. 5, 6).

"And it shall come to pass, when ye be multiplied and increased in the land, in those days, saith the Lord, they shall say no more, The ark of the covenant of the Lord: neither shall it come to mind: neither shall they remember it; neither shall they visit it; neither shall that be done any more.

At that time they shall call Jerusalem the throne of the Lord; and all the nations shall be gathered unto it, to the name of the Lord, to Jerusalem: neither shall they walk any more after the imagination of their evil heart. In those days the house of Judah shall walk with the house of Israel, and they shall come together out of the land of the north to the land that I have given for an inheritance unto your fathers" (*Jer.* iii. 16–18).

" Enlarge the place of thy tent, and let them stretch forth the curtains of thine habitations: spare not, lengthen thy cords, and strengthen thy stakes; for thou shalt break forth on the right hand and on the left; and thy seed shall inherit the Gentiles, and make the desolate cities to be inhabited. Fear not; for thou shalt not be ashamed: neither be thou confounded; for thou shalt not be put to shame: for thou shalt forget the shame of thy youth, and shalt not remember the reproach of thy widowhood any more. For thy Maker is thine husband; the Lord of hosts is his name;

and thy Redeemer the Holy One of Israel ;
the God of the whole earth shall he be
called " (*Isa.* liv. 2–5).

15. PRESENCE OF JEHOVAH.

" The Lord also shall roar out of Zion,
and utter his voice from Jerusalem; and the
heavens and the earth shall shake: but the
Lord will be the hope of his people, and
the strength of the children of Israel. So
shall ye know that I am the Lord your God
dwelling in Zion, my holy mountain; then
shall Jerusalem be holy, and there shall no
strangers pass through her any more " (*Joel*
iii. 16, 17).

" Sing and rejoice, O daughter of Zion:
for, lo, I come, and I will dwell in the
midst of thee, saith the Lord. And many
nations shall be joined to the Lord in that
day, and shall be my people: and I will
dwell in the midst of thee, and thou shalt
know that the Lord of hosts hath sent me
unto thee. And the Lord shall inherit
Judah his portion in the holy land, and
shall choose Jerusalem again. Be silent, O

all flesh, before the Lord, for he is raised up out of his holy habitation" (*Zech.* ii. 10–13).

"According to the word that I cove-nanted with you when ye came out of Egypt, so my spirit remaineth among you: fear ye not. For thus saith the Lord of hosts; Yet once, it is a little while, and I will shake the heavens, and the earth, and the sea, and the dry land; and I will shake all nations, and the desire of all nations shall come: and I will fill this house with glory, saith the Lord of hosts. The silver is mine, and the gold is mine, saith the Lord of hosts. The glory of this latter house shall be greater than of the former, saith the Lord of hosts: and in this place will I give peace, saith the Lord of hosts" (*Hag.* ii. 5–9).

"Look upon Zion, the city of our solem-nities: thine eyes shall see Jerusalem a quiet habitation, a tabernacle that shall not be taken down; not one of the stakes thereof shall ever be removed, neither shall any of the cords thereof be broken. But there the glorious Lord will be unto us a place of broad rivers and streams; wherein shall go no galley with oars, neither shall gallant ship pass thereby. For the Lord is our judge, the Lord is our lawgiver, the Lord is our king ; he will save us" (*Isa.* xxxiii. 20–22).

"And the Lord will create upon every dwelling-place of mount Zion, and upon her assemblies, a cloud and smoke by day, and the shining of a flaming fire by night : for upon all the glory shall be a defence. And there shall be a tabernacle for a shadow in the daytime from the heat, and for a place of refuge, and for a covert from storm and from rain" (*Isa.* iv. 5, 6).

"And in that day shall ye say, Praise the Lord, call upon his name, declare his doings among the people, make mention that his name is exalted. Sing unto the Lord ; for he hath done excellent things : this is known in all the earth. Cry out and shout, thou inhabitant of Zion : for great is the Holy One of Israel in the midst of thee" (*Isa.* xii. 4–6).

"Thus saith the Lord ; I am returned unto Zion, and will dwell in the midst of

Jerusalem: and Jerusalem shall be called a city of truth; and the mountain of the Lord of hosts the holy mountain" (*Zech.* viii. 3).

16. A BLESSING TO THE GENTILES.

"And I will set a sign among them, and I will send those that escape of them unto the nations, to Tarshish, Pul, and Lud, that draw the bow, to Tubal, and Javan, to the isles afar off, that have not heard my fame, neither have seen my glory; and they shall declare my glory among the Gentiles" (*Isa.* lxvi. 19).

"But in the last days it shall come to pass, that the mountain of the house of the Lord shall be established in the top of the mountains, and it shall be exalted above the hills; and people shall flow into it. And many nations shall come, and say, Come, and let us go up to the mountain of the Lord, and to the house of the God of Jacob; and he will teach us of his ways, and we will walk in his paths: for the law shall go forth of Zion, and the word of the Lord from Jerusalem" (*Micah* iv. 1, 2).

"I say then, Have they stumbled that they should fall? God forbid: but rather through their fall salvation is come unto the Gentiles, for to provoke them to jealousy. Now if the fall of them be the riches of the world, and the diminishing of them the riches of the Gentiles; how much more their fulness? For I speak to you Gentiles, inasmuch as I am the apostle of the Gentiles, I magnify mine office: if by any means I may provoke to emulation them which are my flesh, and might save some of them. For if the casting away of them be the reconciling of the world, what shall the receiving of them be, but life from the dead?" (*Rom.* xi. 11–15.)

"For the Lord will have mercy on Jacob, and will yet choose Israel, and set them in their own land: and the strangers shall be joined with them, and they shall cleave to the house of Jacob" (*Isa.* xiv. 1).

"For as the earth bringeth forth her bud, and as the garden causeth the things that are sown in it to spring forth ; so the Lord God will cause righteousness and praise to spring forth before all the nations" (*Isa.* lxi. 11).

"And they that are far off shall come and build in the temple of the Lord" (*Zech.* vi. 15).

"And it shall come to pass, that as ye were a curse among the heathen, O house of Judah, and house of Israel; so will I save you, and ye shall be a blessing" (*Zech.* viii. 13).

"He shall cause them that come of Jacob to take root: Israel shall blossom and. bud, and fill the face of the world with fruit" (*Isa.* xxvii. 6).

17. LENGTH OF DAYS.

"For, behold, I create new heavens and a new earth: and the former shall not be remembered, nor come into mind. But be ye glad and rejoice for ever in that which I create; for, behold, I create Jerusalem a rejoicing, and her people a joy. And I will rejoice in Jerusalem, and joy in my people: and the voice of weeping shall be no more heard in her, nor the voice of

crying. There shall be no more thence an
infant of days, nor an old man that hath
not filled his days: for the child shall die an
hundred years old; but the sinner being an
hundred years old shall be accursed. And
they shall build houses, and inhabit them;
and they shall plant vineyards, and eat the
fruit of them. They shall not build, and
another inhabit; they shall not plant, and
another eat: for, as the days of a tree are
the days of my people, and mine elect shall
long enjoy the work of their hands" (*Isa.*
lxv. 17–22).

18. GLORY.

" Thus saith the Lord, Behold, I will
extend peace to her like a river, and the
glory of the Gentiles like a flowing stream:
then shall ye suck, ye shall be borne upon
her sides, and be dandled upon her knees"
(*Isa.* lxvi. 12).

" Arise, shine; for thy light is come, and
the glory of the Lord is risen upon thee.
For, behold, the darkness shall cover the
earth, and gross darkness the people: but
the Lord shall arise upon thee, and his glory

shall be seen upon thee. And the Gentiles shall come to thy light, and kings to the brightness of thy rising. Lift up thine eyes round about, and see: all they gather themselves together, they come to thee: thy sons shall come from far, and thy daughters shall be nursed at thy side. Then thou shalt see, and flow together, and thine heart shall fear, and be enlarged; because the abundance of the sea shall be converted unto thee, the forces of the Gentiles shall come unto thee. The multitude of camels shall cover thee, the dromedaries of Midian and Ephah; all they from Sheba shall come: they shall bring gold and incense; and they shall show forth the praises of the Lord. All the flocks of Kedar shall be gathered together unto thee, the rams of Nebaioth shall minister unto thee: they shall come up with acceptance on mine altar, and I will glorify the house of my glory" (*Isa.* lx. 1–7).

" For Zion's sake will I not hold my peace, and for Jerusalem's sake I will not rest, until the righteousness thereof go forth as brightness, and the salvation thereof as a lamp that burneth. And the Gentiles shall see thy righteousness, and all kings thy glory: and thou shalt be called by a new name, which the mouth of the Lord shall name. Thou shalt also be a crown of glory in the hand of the Lord, and a royal diadem in the hand of thy God. Thou shalt no more be termed Forsaken; neither shall thy land any more be termed Desolate: but thou shalt be called Hephzibah, and thy land Beulah; for the Lord delighteth in thee, and thy land shall be married. For as a young man marrieth a virgin, so shall thy sons marry thee: and as the bridegroom rejoiceth over the bride, so shall thy God rejoice over thee" (*Isa.* lxii. 1–5).

"O thou afflicted, tossed with tempest, and not comforted, behold, I will lay thy stones with fair colours, and lay thy foundations with sapphires. And I will make thy windows of agates, and thy gates of carbuncles, and all thy borders of pleasant stones" (*Isa.* liv. 11, 12).

"The sun shall be no more thy light by day; neither for brightness shall the moon

give light unto thee: but the Lord shall be
unto thee an everlasting light, and thy God
thy glory. Thy sun shall no more go
down; neither shall thy moon withdraw
itself: for the Lord shall be thine everlasting light, and the days of thy mourning
shall be ended" (*Isa.* lx. 19, 20).

19. FRUITFUL DAYS.

"In that day will I raise up the tabernacle of David that is fallen, and close up
the breaches thereof; and I will raise up his
ruins, and I will build it as in the days of
old: that they may possess the remnant
of Edom, and of all the heathen, which are
called by my name, saith the Lord that
doeth this. Behold, the days come, saith
the Lord, that the plowman shall overtake
the reaper, and the treader of grapes him
that soweth seed; and the mountains shall
drop sweet wine, and all the hills shall
melt" (*Amos* ix. 11–13).

"And it shall come to pass in that day,
that the mountains shall drop down new
wine, and the hills shall flow with milk,

and all the rivers of Judah shall ı
waters, and a fountain shall come
the house of the Lord, and shall water
the valley of Shittim" (*Joel* iii. 18).

"Fear not, O land; be glad and rejoice;
for the Lord will do great things. Be not
afraid, ye beasts of the field: for the pastures
of the wilderness do spring, for the tree
beareth her fruit, the fig tree and the vine
do yield their strength. Be glad then, ye
children of Zion, and rejoice in the Lord
your God: for he hath given you the former
rain moderately, and he will cause to come
down for you the rain, the former rain, and
the latter rain in the first month. And the
floors shall be full of wheat, and the fats
shall overflow with wine and oil. And I
will restore to you the years that the locust
hath eaten, the cankerworm, and the cater-
pillar, and the palmerworm, my great army
which I sent among you. And ye shall eat
in plenty, and be satisfied, and praise the
name of the Lord your God, that hath dealt
wondrously with you: and my people shall
never be ashamed" (*Joel* ii. 21–26).

" But ye, O mountains of Israel, ye shall shoot forth your branches, and yield your fruit to my people of Israel; for they are at hand to come. For, behold, I am for you, and I will turn unto you, and ye shall be tilled and sown: and I will multiply men upon you, all the house of Israel, even all of it: and the cities shall be inhabited, and the wastes shall be builded: and I will multiply upon you man and beast; and they shall increase and bring fruit: and I will settle you after your old estates, and will do better unto you than at your beginnings: and ye shall know that I am the Lord. Yea, I will cause men to walk upon you, even my people Israel; and they shall possess thee, and thou shalt be their inheritance " (*Ezek.* xxxvi. 8–12).

20. GENTILE HELP.

" For the Lord will have mercy on Jacob, and will yet choose Israel, and set them in their own land: and the strangers shall be joined with them, and they shall cleave to the house of Jacob. And the people shall take them, and bring them to their place : and the house of Israel shall possess them in the land of the Lord for servants and handmaids : and they shall take them captives, whose captives they were ; and they shall rule over their oppressors " (*Isa.* xiv. 1, 2).

" Sing and rejoice, O daughter of Zion : for, lo, I come, and I will dwell in the midst of thee, saith the Lord.   And many nations shall be joined to the Lord in that day, and shall be my people : and I will dwell in the midst of thee, and thou shalt know that the Lord of hosts hath sent me unto thee " (*Zech.* ii. 10, 11).

" And kings shall be thy nursing fathers, and their queens thy nursing mothers : they shall bow down to thee with their face toward the earth, and lick up the dust of thy feet ; and thou shalt know that I am the Lord : for they shall not be ashamed that wait for me " (*Isa.* xlix. 23).

21. REGATHERING.

" Behold, I will gather them out of all countries, whither I have driven them in mine anger, and in my fury, and in great wrath; and I will bring them again unto this place, and I will cause them to dwell safely: and they shall be my people, and I will be their God: and I will give them one heart, and one way, that they may fear me for ever, for the good of them, and of their children after them: and I will make an everlasting covenant with them, that I will not turn away from them, to do them good; but I will put my fear in their hearts, that they shall not depart from me." (*Jer.* xxxii. 37–40).

" Hear the word of the Lord, O ye nations, and declare it in the isles afar off, and say, He that scattered Israel will gather him, and keep him, as a shepherd doth his flock. For the Lord hath redeemed Jacob, and ransomed him from the hand of him that was stronger than he. Therefore they shall come and sing in the height of Zion, and shall flow together to the goodness of the Lord, for wheat, and for wine, and for oil, and for the young of the flock and of the herd: and their soul shall be as a watered garden ; and they shall not sorrow any more at all" (*Jer.* xxxi. 10–12).

" In that time shall the present be brought unto the Lord of hosts of a people scattered and peeled, and from a people terrible from their beginning hitherto; a nation meted out and trodden under foot, whose land the rivers have spoiled, to the place of the name of the Lord of hosts, the mount Zion" (*Isa.* xviii. 7).

" And it shall come to pass in that day, that the Lord shall set his hand again the second time to recover the remnant of his people, which shall be left, from Assyria, and from Egypt, and from Pathros, and from Cush, and from Elam, and from Shinar, and from Hamath, and from the islands of the sea. And he shall set up an ensign for the nations, and shall assemble the outcasts of Israel, and gather together the dispersed of Judah from the four corners of the earth" (*Isa.* xi. 11, 12).

" I will sanctify my great name, which was profaned among the heathen, which ye have profaned in the midst of them; and the heathen shall know that I am the Lord, saith the Lord God, when I shall be sanctified in you before their eyes. For I will take you from among the heathen, and gather you out of all countries, and will bring you into your own land" (*Ezek.* xxxvi. 22–24).

22. PERPETUITY.

"Thus saith the Lord, which giveth the sun for a light by day, and the ordinances of the moon and of the stars for a light by night, which divideth the sea when the waves thereof roar; the Lord of hosts is his name: If those ordinances depart from before me, saith the Lord, then the seed of Israel also shall cease from being a nation before me for ever. Thus saith the Lord; If heaven above can be measured, and the foundations of the earth searched out beneath, I will also cast off all the seed of Israel for all that they have done, saith the Lord" (*Jer.* xxxi. 35–37).

"For as the new heavens and the new

earth, which I will make, shall remain before me, saith the Lord, so shall your seed and your name remain" (*Isa.* lxvi. 22).

" Whereas thou hast been forsaken and hated, so that no man went through thee, I will make thee an eternal excellency, a joy of many generations" (*Isa.* lx. 15).

" The children of thy servants shall continue, and their seed shall be established before thee" (*Ps.* cii. 28).

" Judah shall dwell for ever, and Jerusalem from generation to generation" (*Joel* iii. 20).

23. DIVINE FAVOUR.

" I say then, Hath God cast away his people? God forbid. For I also am an Israelite, of the seed of Abraham, of the tribe of Benjamin. God hath not cast away his people which he foreknew. Wot ye not what the Scripture saith of Elias? how he maketh intercession to God against Israel, saying, Lord, they have killed thy prophets, and digged down thine altars; and I am left alone, and they seek my life. But what saith the answer of God unto him? I have reserved to myself seven thousand men, who have not bowed the knee to the image of Baal. Even so then at this present time also there is a remnant according to the election of grace" (*Rom.* xi. 1–5).

"Yet the number of the children of Israel shall be as the sand of the sea, which cannot be measured nor numbered; and it shall come to pass, that in the place where it was said unto them, Ye are not my people, there it shall be said unto them, Ye are the sons of the living God" (*Hosea* i. 10).

"How goodly are thy tents, O Jacob! and thy tabernacles, O Israel! As the valleys are they spread forth, as gardens by the river's side, as the trees of lign aloes, which the Lord hath planted, and as cedar trees beside the waters. He shall pour the water out of his buckets, and his seed shall be in many waters; and his king shall be higher than Agag, and his kingdom shall be exalted" (*Num.* xxiv. 5–7).

CHAPTER V.

FOR THE WORLD.

THOUGH many of the promises to the sinner individually belong to the world at large, and many of the promises to the world apply to the sinner personally, yet it is of some importance to gather together the words of grace in which God has spoken to "the world," to "all nations," to the "Gentiles" who are "afar off," as well as to the Jews who are "nigh."

When meeting some Bedawi of the Arabian desert, or some fellah of Syria, or some unwashed, tattered drunkard of our great cities, we are apt to look on them as hopeless fragments of humanity, too far gone in ignorance or sin even for pity,—

> "Waifs in the universe, the last
> Lorn links of kindred chains for ever sundered,"

we seem almost persuaded that these outcasts are as much overlooked by God as by man.

"They as some atom seem, which God
Had made superfluously and needed not
To build creation with; but back again
To nothing threw, and left it in the void,
With everlasting sense that once it was."

But the large and wide words of Scripture take up all these wanderers; so that one in reading them feels that there is no outcast here too far gone astray to be brought back, or too deeply sunk in crime to be drawn out, or too thoroughly lost in the multitude to be singled out by the eye or yearned over by the heart of God. He who makes his sun to rise and his rain to fall on such, has not forgotten them, though his manner of dealing with them may seem a mystery to us.

We take this expression, "the world," as referring to the race of men and to the earth which was made for them at first, and of which they were commanded to have dominion. To the far-off Gentile, to the very "ends of the earth," the gospel goes forth in its free gladness; and that word "whosoever" is an expression of the widest compass. "Whosoever will" says the message.

The world's future will show how widely the glad tidings were meant to go. "Preach the gospel to every creature" is our commission now; and though we wonder and mourn at the reception it meets with, and say, "Who hath believed our report? and to whom is the arm of the Lord revealed?" yet there is hope, and God's word of promise points us to a future as bright as the past has been dark both for creation and its inhabitants. Into the details of that future we do not enter. Let our readers betake themselves to the word itself. We give but a slender selection of promises on this head. A larger one would be out of place here, and a complete one would require a volume.

The kingdoms of this world are to become the kingdoms of our Lord and of his Christ; and he who is, even now, "the Prince of the kings of the earth," shall take to himself his great power and reign. Then it shall no more be said, "the whole world lieth in wickedness." Satan shall no longer be the "god of this world," the "prince of this world," nor shall his "principalities and powers" be "the rulers of the darkness of this world." "This present evil world" shall then be forgotten in the holiness of that which is to come. To this period many a promise points, and as our security we have the Father's purpose, in the development of which the whole world is interested. Into the nature of that purpose, or the details of that development, we do not enter, further than by collecting and classifying the promises of Scripture concerning the world's future.

1. GOOD NEWS FOR THE WORLD.

" And suddenly there was with the angel a multitude of the heavenly host praising God, and saying, Glory to God in the highest, and on earth peace, good will toward men " (*Luke* ii. 13, 14).

" And he said unto them, Go ye into all the world, and preach the gospel to every creature " (*Mark* xvi. 15).

" And this gospel of the kingdom shall be preached in all the world for a witness unto all nations; and then shall the end come" (*Matt*. xxiv. 14).

" And Jesus came and spake unto them, saying, All power is given unto me in heaven and in earth. Go ye therefore, and teach all nations, baptizing them in the name of the Father, and of the Son, and of the Holy Ghost : teaching them to observe all things whatsoever I have commanded you : and, lo, I am with you alway, even unto the end of the world. Amen " (*Matt.* xxviii. 18–20).

" And we have seen and do testify that the Father sent the Son to be the Saviour of the world. Whosoever shall confess that Jesus is the Son of God, God dwelleth in him, and he in God. And we have known and believed the love that God hath to us. God is love; and he that dwelleth in love, dwelleth in God, and God in him " (1 *John* iv. 14–16).

" And I saw another angel fly in the midst of heaven, having the everlasting gospel to preach unto them that dwell on the earth, and to every nation, and kindred, and tongue, and people, saying with a loud voice, Fear God, and give glory to him; for the hour of his judgment is come: and worship him that made heaven, and earth, and the sea, and the fountains of waters " (*Rev.* xiv. 6, 7).

" To whom God would make known what is the riches of the glory of this mystery among the Gentiles; which is Christ in you, the hope of glory " (*Col.* i. 27).

2. LIGHT FOR THE WORLD.

" That was the true Light, which lighteth every man that cometh into the world. He was in the world, and the world was made by him, and the world knew him not. He came unto his own, and his own received him not. But as many as received him, to them gave he power to become the sons of God, even to them that believe on his name: which were born, not of blood, nor of the will of the flesh, nor of the will of man, but of God " (*John* i. 9–13).

" Jesus cried and said, He that believeth on me, believeth not on me, but on him that sent me. And he that seeth me seeth him that sent me. I am come a light into the world, that whosoever believeth on me should not abide in darkness. And if any man hear my words, and believe not, I judge him not: for I came not to judge the world, but to save the world " (*John* xii. 44–47).

" Then spake Jesus again unto them saying, I am the light of the world: he that followeth me shall not walk in darkness, but shall have the light of life" (*John* viii. 12).

"And thou, child, shalt be called the prophet of the Highest: for thou shalt go before the face of the Lord to prepare his ways; to give knowledge of salvation unto his people, by the remission of their sins, through the tender mercy of our God; whereby the dayspring from on high hath visited us, to give light to them that sit in darkness and in the shadow of death, to guide our feet into the way of peace" (*Luke* i. 76–79).

"For mine eyes have seen thy salvation, which thou hast prepared before the face of all people; a light to lighten the Gentiles, and the glory of thy people Israel" (*Luke* ii. 30–32).

"The darkness is past, and the true light now shineth" (1 *John* ii. 8).

3. BREAD FOR THE WORLD.

"For the bread of God is he which cometh down from heaven, and giveth life unto the world. Then said they unto him,

Lord, evermore give us this bread. And Jesus said unto them, I am the bread of life : he that cometh to me shall never hunger ; and he that believeth on me shall never thirst" (*John* vi. 33–35).

"And when he came to himself, he said, How many hired servants of my father's have bread enough and to spare, and I perish with hunger ! I will arise and go to my father, and will say unto him, Father, I have sinned against heaven, and before thee, and am no more worthy to be called thy son : make me as one of thy hired servants. And he arose, and came to his father. But when he was yet a great way off, his father saw him, and had compassion, and ran, and fell on his neck, and kissed him. And the son said unto him, Father, I have sinned against heaven, and in thy sight, and am no more worthy to be called thy son. But the father said to his servants, Bring forth the best robe, and put it on him ; and put a ring on his hand, and shoes on his feet: and bring hither the fatted calf, and kill it ; and let us eat, and be merry : for this my son was dead, and is alive again; he was lost, and is found. And they began to be merry" (*Luke* xv. 17–24).

"Go out quickly into the streets and lanes of the city, and bring in hither the poor, and the maimed, and the halt, and the blind. And the servant said, Lord, it is done as thou hast commanded, and yet there is room. And the lord said unto the servant, Go out into the highways and hedges, and compel them to come in, that my house may be filled" (*Luke* xiv. 21–23).

4. LIFE FOR THE WORLD.

"For God so loved the world, that he gave his only begotten Son, that whosoever believeth in him should not perish, but have everlasting life. For God sent not his Son into the world to condemn the world; but that the world through him might be saved" (*John* iii. 16, 17).

"As the Father knoweth me, even so know I the Father: and I lay down my life for the sheep. And other sheep I have, which are not of this fold : them also I must bring, and they shall hear my voice ; and there shall be one fold and one shepherd. Therefore doth my Father love me, because I lay down my life, that I might take it again.   No man taketh it from me, but I lay it down of myself.   I have power to lay it down, and I have power to take it again. This commandment have I received of my Father " (*John* x. 15–18).

" In this was manifested the love of God toward us, because that God sent his only begotten Son into the world, that we might live through him.   Herein is love, not that we loved God, but that he loved us, and sent his Son to be the propitiation for our sin" (1 *John* iv. 9, 10).

5. HEALING FOR THE WORLD.

" And as Moses lifted up the serpent in the wilderness, even so must the Son of man be lifted up : that whosoever believeth in him should not perish, but have eternal life" (*John* iii. 14, 15).

" And he showed me a pure river of water of life, clear as crystal, proceeding out of the throne of God and of the Lamb. In the midst of the street of it, and on either side of the river, was there the tree of life, which bare twelve manner of fruits, and yielded her fruit every month : and the leaves of the tree were for the healing of the nations " (*Rev.* xxii. 1, 2).

" And he said unto me, Son of man, hast thou seen this ? Then he brought me, and caused me to return to the brink of the river. Now when I had returned, behold, at the bank of the river were very many trees on the one side and on the other. Then said he unto me, These waters issue out toward the east country, and go down into the desert, and go into the sea : which being brought forth into the sea, the waters shall be healed. And it shall come to pass, that everything that liveth, which moveth, whithersoever the rivers shall come, shall live : and there shall be a very great multitude of fish, because these waters shall come thither : for they shall be healed ; and every thing shall live whither the river cometh. . . . And by the river upon the bank thereof, on this side and on that side, shall grow all trees for meat, whose leaf shall not fade, neither shall the fruit thereof be consumed: it shall bring forth new fruit according to his months, because their waters they issued out of the sanctuary: and the fruit thereof shall be for meat, and the leaf thereof for medicine" (*Ezek.* xlvii. 6–9, 12).

6. CREATION'S DELIVERANCE.

"For the earnest expectation of the creature waiteth for the manifestation of the sons of God. For the creature was made subject to vanity, not willingly, but by reason of him who hath subjected the same in hope, because the creature itself also shall be delivered from the bondage of corruption into the glorious liberty of the children of God. For we know that the whole creation groaneth and travaileth in pain together until now. And not only they, but ourselves also, which have the firstfruits of the Spirit, even we ourselves groan within ourselves, waiting for the adoption, to wit, the redemption of our body" (*Rom.* viii. 19–23).

"And it shall come to pass in that day, that the Lord shall punish the host of the high ones that are on high, and the kings of the earth upon the earth. And they shall be gathered together, as prisoners are gathered in the pit, and shall be shut up in the prison, and after many days shall they be visited. Then the moon shall be confounded, and the sun ashamed, when the Lord of hosts shall reign in mount Zion, and in Jerusalem, and before his ancients gloriously" (*Isa.* xxiv. 21–23).

"Repent ye therefore, and be converted, that your sins may be blotted out, when the times of refreshing shall come from the presence of the Lord; and he shall send Jesus Christ, which before was preached unto you: whom the heaven must receive until the times of restitution of all things, which God hath spoken by the mouth of all his holy prophets since the world began" (*Acts* iii. 19–21).

" Behold, a king shall reign in righteousness, and princes shall rule in judgment. And a man shall be as an hiding-place from the wind, and a covert from the tempest; as rivers of water in a dry place, as the shadow of a great rock in a weary land. And the eyes of them that see shall not be dim, and the ears of them that hear shall hearken. The heart also of the rash shall understand knowledge, and the tongue of the stammerers shall be ready to speak plainly. The vile person shall be no more called liberal, nor the churl said to be bountiful " (*Isa.* xxxii. 1–5).

" Give the king thy judgments, O God, and thy righteousness unto the king's son. He shall judge thy people with righteousness, and thy poor with judgment. The mountains shall bring peace to the people, and the little hills, by righteousness. He shall judge the poor of the people, he shall save the children of the needy, and shall break in pieces the oppressor. They shall fear thee as long as the sun and moon endure, throughout all generations. He shall

come down like rain upon the mown grass:
as showers that water the earth. In his
days shall the righteous flourish; and
abundance of peace so long as the moon
endureth. He shall have dominion also
from sea to sea, and from the river unto
the ends of the earth. They that dwell
in the wilderness shall bow before him;
and his enemies shall lick the dust. The
kings of Tarshish and of the isles shall
bring presents: the kings of Sheba and
Seba shall offer gifts. Yea, all kings shall
fall down before him: all nations shall
serve him. For he shall deliver the needy
when he crieth; the poor also, and him that
hath no helper. He shall spare the poor
and needy, and shall save the souls of the
needy. He shall redeem their soul from
deceit and violence: and precious shall their
blood be in his sight. And he shall live,
and to him shall be given of the gold of
Sheba: prayer also shall be made for him
continually; and daily shall he be praised"
(*Ps.* lxxii. 1–15).

7. CREATION'S GLADNESS.

" Make a joyful noise unto the Lord, all the earth : make a loud noise, and rejoice, and sing praise. Sing unto the Lord with the harp; with the harp, and the voice of a psalm. With trumpets and sound of cornet make a joyful noise before the Lord, the King. Let the sea roar, and the fulness thereof; the world, and they that dwell therein. Let the floods clap their hands : let the hills be joyful together before the Lord ; for he cometh to judge the earth : with righteousness shall he judge the world, and the people with equity " (*Ps.* xcviii. 4–9).

" O worship the Lord in the beauty of holiness : fear before him, all the earth. Say among the heathen that the Lord reigneth : the world also shall be established that it shall not be moved : he shall judge the people righteously. Let the heavens rejoice, and let the earth be glad; let the sea roar, and the fulness thereof. Let the field be joyful, and all that is therein : then shall

all the trees of the wood rejoice before the Lord: for he cometh, for he cometh to judge the earth" (*Ps.* xcvi. 9–13).

" There shall be an handful of corn in the earth upon the top of the mountains; the fruit thereof shall shake like Lebanon: and they of the city shall flourish like grass of the earth. His name shall endure for ever: his name shall be continued as long as the sun: and men shall be blessed in him: all. nations shall call him blessed. Blessed be the Lord God, the God of Israel, who only doeth wondrous things. And blessed be his glorious name for ever: and let the whole earth be filled with his glory; Amen, and Amen" (*Ps.* lxxii. 16–19).

"God be merciful unto us, and bless us; and cause his face to shine upon us; Selah; that thy way may be known upon earth, thy saving health among all nations. Let the people praise thee, O God; let all the people praise thee. O let the nations be glad and sing for joy: for thou shalt judge the people righteously, and govern the nations upon earth. Selah. Let the people

praise thee, O God; let all the people praise
thee. Then shall the earth yield her increase; and God, even our own God, shall
bless us. God shall bless us; and all the
ends of the earth shall fear him" (*Ps.* lxvii.
1–7).

"Sing unto the Lord a new song, and
his praise from the end of the earth, ye that
go down to the sea, and all that is therein;
the isles, and the inhabitants thereof. Let
the wilderness and the cities thereof lift up
their voice, the villages that Kedar doth
inhabit: let the inhabitants of the rock sing,
let them shout from the top of the mountains. Let them give glory unto the Lord,
and declare his praise in the islands" (*Isa.*
xlii. 10–12).

"Let the heavens be glad, and let the earth
rejoice: and let men say among the nations,
The Lord reigneth. Let the sea roar, and
the fulness thereof: let the fields rejoice,
and all that is therein. Then shall the
trees of the wood sing out at the presence of
the Lord, because he cometh to judge the
earth" (1 *Chron.* xvi. 31–33).

8. CREATION'S REFRESHMENT

" Until the Spirit be poured upon us from on high, and the wilderness be a fruitful field, and the fruitful field be counted for a forest. Then judgment shall dwell in the wilderness, and righteousness remain in the fruitful field. And the work of righteousness shall be peace: and the effect of righteousness quietness and assurance for ever. And my people shall dwell in a peaceable habitation, and in sure dwellings, and in quiet resting-places " (*Isa.* xxxii. 15-18).

" For ye shall go out with joy, and be led forth with peace: the mountains and the hills shall break forth before you into singing, and all the trees of the field shall clap their hands. Instead of the thorn shall come up the fir tree, and instead of the brier shall come up the myrtle tree: and it shall be to the Lord for a name, for an everlasting sign that shall not be cut off" (*Isa.* lv. 12, 13).

" And there shall be no more curse: but

the throne of God and of the Lamb shall be in it; and his servants shall serve him: and they shall see his face; and his name shall be in their foreheads. And there shall be no night there" (*Rev.* xxii. 3–5).

"Now these be the last words of David. David the son of Jesse said, and the man who was raised up on high, the anointed of the God of Jacob, and the sweet psalmist of Israel, said, The Spirit of the Lord spake by me, and his word was in my tongue. The God of Israel said, the Rock of Israel spake to me, He that ruleth over men must be just, ruling in the fear of God. And he shall be as the light of the morning, when the sun riseth, even a morning without clouds; as the tender grass springing out of the earth by clear shining after rain. Although my house be not so with God; yet he hath made with me an everlasting covenant, ordered in all things, and sure: for this is all my salvation, and all my desire, although he make it not to grow" (2 *Sam.* xxiii. 1–5).

CHAPTER VI.

SPECIAL CASES AND PERSONS.

THERE are special classes to whom special promises are made, according to their earthly circumstances. For such is the grace of our God, and such the varied fulness of his word, that every case that can occur amongst us has been considered, and cared for, and spoken to. Truly his tender mercies are over all his works ; he openeth his hand and supplieth the wants of every living thing. He not only numbers and names the stars, but he counts the hairs of our head ; he notes the sparrows ; he feeds the young lions and the ravens. The little things of earth are great to him ; and there is no creature too small for him to notice, or to use, or to bless. The great ones of earth proudly show their greatness by caring for what is great, and overlooking what is little. The great Jehovah shows his greatness by attending to the least and meanest objects in creation. Poverty, weakness, obscurity, low-liness, disease, are to him no repellents, but

attractives.   The peculiar cases that have no
help nor care from man are those which the
God of majesty and glory delights to recognise
and care for.   And just as no sin, however
small, escapes his notice, so no sorrow, however hidden, escapes his sympathy.   There is
significance in that text, "In him we live, and
move, and have our being," as profound as it
is comforting.

1. The Poor and Needy.

It is want that draws us to him who can
supply it ; and it is this same want that draws
him to us.   With men it is the like that come
together, with God it is the unlike ; for with
him it is poverty that attracts riches; and
emptiness, fulness; and sickness, health.   This
is true in every sense.   Hence God has inti-
mated to us, once and again, his special care
for the poor, for in the poor man God finds
his fullest opportunity of unfolding and be-
stowing all his riches.   It was to poverty that
the Son of God descended ; he stooped to the
estate of the poor man, of one who had not
even where to lay his head.   He can sym-
pathize with human poverty, and with all
the privations and inconveniences to which
poverty exposes men.   It was with the poor

man's dwelling that he was familiar; it was the poor man's lot that he experienced here. O human poverty, thou art not uncared for and unblest! Ye poor of earth, God is calling you to the fellowship of his Son, and to the heavenly riches!

" Thou hast been a strength to the poor, a strength to the needy in his distress" (*Isa.* xxv. 4).

" This poor man cried, and the Lord heard him, and saved him out of all his troubles" (*Ps.* xxxiv. 6).

" Hath not God chosen the poor of this world rich in faith, and heirs of the kingdom which he hath promised to them that love him?" (*James* ii. 5).

" The poor have the gospel preached to them" (*Matt.* xi. 5).

" He hath delivered the soul of the poor from the hand of evildoers" (*Jer.* xx. 13).

" With righteousness shall he judge the poor" (*Isa.* xi. 4).

" He that hath mercy on the poor, happy is he" (*Prov.* xiv. 21).

" I know that the Lord will maintain the cause of the afflicted, and the right of the poor " (*Ps.* cxl. 12).

" He shall stand at the right hand of the poor " (*Ps.* cix. 31).

" He setteth the poor on high from affliction " (*Ps.* cvii. 41).

" He shall judge the poor of the people, he shall save the children of the needy " (*Ps.* lxxii. 4).

" The Lord heareth the poor " (*Ps.* lxix. 33).

" Thou, O God, hast prepared of thy goodness for the poor " (*Ps.* lxviii. 10).

" The expectation of the poor shall not perish for ever " (*Ps.* ix. 18).

2. THE OLD.

Old age is not overlooked by God; and the man that has toiled through life's years of care and trial till his hairs are grey is not forgotten. "The Ancient of days" takes the aged of Adam's sons under his special care; and he with whom one day is as a thousand years, numbers in love our threescore years and ten. Were they not his own thoughts and feelings that he expressed when he said, "The hoary head is a crown of glory;" and again, "Thou shalt rise up before the hoary head, and honour the face of the old man"? (Lev. xix. 32.)

"They shall still bring forth fruit in old age; they shall be fat and flourishing" (*Ps.* xcii. 14).

"Even to your old age I am he; and even to hoar hairs will I carry you: I have made, and I will bear; even I will carry, and will deliver you" (*Isa.* xlvi. 4).

3. THE YOUNG.

Though God says, "Childhood and youth are vanity," he does not do so as if he cared not for the young. He loves them; he yearns over them; and he grieves to see them wasting the fresh days of childhood and filling their hearts with that which will bring them no gladness. "Suffer the little children to come to me" is the voice of the Old as well as the New Testament. Remember thy Creator in the days of thy youth. Be Samuels, be Josiahs, be Timothys. Begin early with the love of God, and your lives will be true and noble, as well as blessed.

"Wilt thou not from this time cry unto me, My Father, thou art the guide of my youth?" (*Jer.* iii. 4).

"I love them that love me; and those that seek me early shall find me" (*Prov.* viii. 17).

"Come, ye children, hearken unto me: I will teach you the fear of the Lord" (*Ps.* xxxiv. 11).

"I will pour my Spirit upon thy seed, and my blessing upon thine offspring: and they shall spring up as among the grass, as willows by the water-courses" (*Isa.* xliv. 3, 4).

"Honour thy father and thy mother: that thy days may be long upon the land which the Lord thy God giveth thee (*Ex.* xx. 12).

"Thy children shall be like olive plants round about thy table" (*Ps.* cxxviii. 3).

"All thy children shall be taught of the Lord; and great shall be the peace of thy children" (*Isa.* liv. 13).

4. THE SICK.

It is the sick that need the physician; and it was as the physician that God announced himself to Israel. "I am the Lord that healeth thee" (Exod. xv. 26). It was as the pitier and healer of the sick that the Son of God came to earth. "He went about healing all manner of sicknesses and diseases." A sick bed, then, is just the place where we may expect to meet with Jesus. Sick and pained ones of earth, Jesus pities you. Deal directly with him about your case; and if he does not heal you, he will give you something better than healing.

" Jesus went about all Galilee, healing all manner of sickness and all manner of disease among the people. And his fame went throughout all Syria; and they brought unto him all sick people that were taken with divers diseases and torments, and those which were possessed with devils, and those which were lunatic, and those that had the palsy; and he healed them" (*Matt.* iv. 23, 24).

" The inhabitant shall not say, I am sick:

the people that dwell therein shall be forgiven their iniquity " (*Isa.* xxxiii. 24).

" I will bind up that which was broken, and will strengthen that which was sick " (*Ezek.* xxxiv. 16).

" Is any sick among you, let him call for the elders of the church ; and let them pray over him, anointing him with oil in the name of the Lord : and the prayer of faith shall save the sick, and the Lord shall raise him up ; and if he have committed sins, they shall be forgiven him " (*James* v. 14).

" I kill, and I make alive ; I wound, and I heal " (*Deut.* xxxii. 39).

" Jesus saith unto him, I will come and heal him " (*Matt.* viii. 7).

" Strengthen ye the weak hands, and confirm the feeble knees. The eyes of the blind shall be opened, and the ears of the deaf shall be unstopped. Then shall the lame man leap as an hart, and the tongue of the dumb sing " (*Isa.* xxxv. 3, 5, 6).

" O Lord my God, I cried unto thee, and thou hast healed me. O Lord, thou hast brought up my soul from the grave: thou hast kept me alive, that I should not go down to the pit" (*Ps.* xxx. 2, 3).

"The leaves of the tree were for the healing of the nations" (*Rev.* xxii. 2).

5. THE WIDOWS.

To all kinds of weakness, want, and sorrow, God stretches out his pitying hands. He delights to bind up breaches, to fill up blanks, to comfort the troubled, to cheer broken hearts. He has taken the widow under his special care, and has made her feel that whoever may desert her, God will not. He is the widow's God, and speaks as such to the widowed soul of every nation and age. It was to the widows (not of Israel, but of Edom) that he said, "Let thy widows trust in me" (Jer. xlix. 11).

"The Lord your God is God of gods, and Lord of lords, a great God, a mighty, and a terrible, which regardeth not persons, nor taketh reward: he doth execute the judgment of the fatherless and widow, and loveth the stranger" (*Deut.* x. 17, 18).

"The sheaf in the field shall be for the

stranger, for the fatherless, and for the widow" (*Deut.* xxiv. 19).

"He relieveth the fatherless and the widow" (*Ps.* cxlvi. 9).

"He will establish the border of the widow" (*Prov.* xv. 25).

"A judge of the widows is God in his holy habitation" (*Ps.* lxviii. 5).

"Pure religion and undefiled before God and the Father is this, To visit the fatherless and widows in their affliction" (*James* i. 27).

6. The Fatherless.

They from whom an earthly father has been taken, find shelter under the wing of a Father in heaven. To orphanage he shows special care and pity; all the more because it is he himself who, in his wise love, has taken the earthly parent away. O fatherless children, look up and be of good cheer. Learn to say, Abba, Father.

"Ye shall not afflict any widow, or fatherless child. If thou afflict them in any wise, and they cry at all unto me, I will surely hear their cry; and my wrath shall wax hot, and I will kill you with the sword; and your wives shall be widows, and your children fatherless" (*Ex.* xxii. 22–24).

"He doth execute the judgment of the fatherless and widow, and loveth the stranger, in giving him food and raiment" (*Deut.* x. 18).

"Thou hast seen it; for thou beholdest mischief and spite, to requite it with thy hand: the poor committeth himself unto thee; thou art the helper of the fatherless" (*Ps.* x. 14).

"A father of the fatherless, and a judge of the widows, is God in his holy habitation" (*Ps.* lxviii. 5).

"Remove not the old landmark; and enter not into the fields of the fatherless: for their redeemer is mighty; he shall plead their cause with thee" (*Prov.* xxiii. 10, 11).

"Leave thy fatherless children, I will preserve them alive; and let thy widows trust in me" (*Jer.* xlix. 11).

"In thee the fatherless findeth mercy" (*Hosea* xiv. 3).

7. THE OPPRESSED.

"The righteous Lord loveth righteousness," is God's character of himself. Yes; he is good, and loveth goodness; he is kind, and loveth kindness; he is generous, and loveth generosity; he is pitiful, and loveth pity. So also he hateth injustice, cruelty, slavery, oppression, extortion, and all unfairness or unkindness between man. In him, the captive, the slave, the oppressed, the injured, find sympathy.

"It shall come to pass, when he crieth unto me, I will hear; for I am gracious" *Ex.* xxii. 27).

"He shall judge the poor of the people, he shall save the children of the needy, and shall break in pieces the oppressor" (*Ps.* lxxii. 4).

"For the oppression of the poor, for the sighing of the needy, now will I arise, saith the Lord; I will set him in safety from him that puffeth at him" (*Ps.* xii. 5).

"The Lord also will be a refuge for the oppressed, a refuge in times of trouble.

And they that know thy name will put their trust in thee: for thou, Lord, hast not forsaken them that seek thee" (*Ps.* ix. 9, 10).

8. The Stranger.

We use the word in the common sense; of one away from home, in a foreign land. God pities such, and has commanded us to care for such. His tender mercies are over all his works; and while Israel was, no doubt, his peculiar people, he did not overlook the Gentile stranger, "nor would he allow his people to do so; for God is love, and he that dwelleth in love, dwelleth in God, and God in him."

"Thou shalt neither vex a stranger, nor oppress him: for ye were strangers in the land of Egypt" (*Ex.* xxii. 21).

"Also thou shalt not oppress a stranger: for ye know the heart of a stranger, seeing ye were strangers in the land of Egypt" (*Ex.* xxiii. 9).

"He doth execute the judgment of the fatherless and widow, and loveth the stranger, in giving him food and raiment. Love ye

therefore the stranger : for ye were strangers
in the land of Egypt" (*Deut.* x. 18, 19).

" Be not forgetful to entertain strangers :
for thereby some have entertained angels
unawares" (*Heb.* xiii. 2).

" The Lord preserveth the strangers ; he
relieveth the fatherless and widow : but the
way of the wicked he turneth upside down"
(*Ps.* cxlvi. 9).

" And it shall come to pass, that ye shall
divide it by lot for an inheritance unto
you, and to the strangers that sojourn among
you, which shall beget children among you :
and they shall be unto you as born in the
country among the children of Israel ; they
shall have inheritance with you among the
tribes of Israel.   And it shall come to pass,
that in what tribe the stranger sojourneth,
there shall ye give him his inheritance, saith
the Lord God" (*Ezek.* xlvii. 22, 23).

9. SERVANTS.

The Son of God was himself a servant; he
came not to be served, but to serve, and to
give his life a ransom for many.   He took

the servant's place; he took upon him the form of a servant; he was the Father's servant for us. As such he knows a servant's heart, and gives his sympathy to such.

"Art thou called being a servant? care not for it: but if thou mayest be made free, use it rather. For he that is called in the Lord, being a servant, is the Lord's freeman: likewise also he that is called, being free, is Christ's servant" (1 *Cor.* vii. 21, 22).

"Let as many servants as are under the yoke count their own masters worthy of all honour, that the name of God and his doctrine be not blasphemed. And they that have believing masters, let them not despise them, because they are brethren; but rather do them service, because they are faithful and beloved, partakers of the benefit. These things teach and exhort" (1 *Tim.* vi. 1, 2).

"He that is greatest among you, let him be as the younger; and he that is chief, as he that doth serve. For whether is greater, he that sitteth at meat, or he that serveth?

is not he that sitteth at meat? but I am among you as he that serveth" (*Luke* xxii. 26, 27).

"Servants, be obedient to them that are your masters according to the flesh, with fear and trembling, in singleness of your heart, as unto Christ; not with eyeservice, as menpleasers; but as the servants of Christ, doing the will of God from the heart; with good will doing service, as to the Lord, and not to men: knowing that whatsoever good thing any man doeth, the same shall he receive of the Lord, whether he be bond or free" (*Eph.* vi. 5–8).

10. CAPTIVES AND PRISONERS.

God looks into the prison as well as the palace, and he pities the prisoner. He remembers Joseph and Jeremiah; and he does not forget the loneliness and weariness of one, like them, in the low dungeon. His compassions are infinite.

"The Lord looseth the prisoners" (*Ps.* cxlvi. 7).

"To proclaim liberty to the captives,

and the opening of the prison to them that are bound" (*Isa.* lxi. 1).

"He bringeth out those which are bound with chains: but the rebellious dwell in a dry land" (*Ps.* lxviii. 6).

"Such as sit in darkness and in the shadow of death, being bound in affliction and iron; because they rebelled against the words of God, and contemned the counsel of the most High: therefore he brought down their heart with labour; they fell down, and there was none to help. Then they cried unto the Lord in their trouble, and he saved them out of their distresses. He brought them out of darkness and the shadow of death, and brake their bands in sunder" (*Ps.* cvii. 10–14).

"The Lord heareth the poor, and despiseth not his prisoners" (*Ps.* lxix. 33).

11. THE CHILDLESS.

God has, in his word, and in all his dealings, recognised children as blessings, and the want of them as a sore calamity. Hence he speaks words of compassion to those from whom children have been taken, or to whom none had been given. God, the God of Abraham, Isaac, and Jacob, speaks in love to his Rachels, who, in bitterness of spirit, cry, "Give me children, or else I die."

"God setteth the solitary in families" (*Ps.* lxviii. 6).

"He maketh the barren woman to keep house, and to be a joyful mother of children" (*Ps.* cxiii. 9).

"Thus saith the Lord unto the eunuchs that keep my sabbaths, and choose the things that please me, and take hold of my covenant; even unto them will I give in mine house and within my walls a place and a name better than of sons and of daughters : I will give them an everlasting name, that shall not be cut off" (*Isa.* lvi. 4, 5).

12. The Blind, and Deaf, and Lame.

God has no pleasure in the marring of any part of his work. He marks each defect, and though he does not remove it now, he does not the less pity those who are suffering under it. He notices each wound, each pain, each want; and he sends messages of love to the blind, and the deaf, and the halt, and the suffering.

" Thou shalt not curse the deaf, nor put a stumbling-block before the blind, but shalt fear thy God: I am the Lord " (*Lev.* xix. 14).

" Cursed be he that maketh the blind to wander out of the way. And all the people shall say, Amen " (*Deut.* xxvii. 18).

" Which executeth judgment for the oppressed: which giveth food to the hungry. The Lord looseth the prisoners: the Lord openeth the eyes of the blind: the Lord raiseth them that are bowed down: the Lord loveth the righteous" (*Ps.* cxlvi. 7, 8).

" And in that day shall the deaf hear the words of the book, and the eyes of the blind shall see out of obscurity, and out of darkness " (*Isa.* xxix. 18).

" Then the eyes of the blind shall be opened, and the ears of the deaf shall be unstopped. Then shall the lame man leap as an hart, and the tongue of the dumb sing " (*Isa.* xxxv. 5, 6).

" I will bring them from the north country, and gather them from the coasts of the earth, and with them the blind and the lame, the woman with child and her that travaileth with child together : a great company shall return thither " (*Jer.* xxxi. 8).

" And he cometh to Bethsaida ; and they bring a blind man unto him, and besought him to touch him. And he took the blind man by the hand, and led him out of the town ; and when he had spit on his eyes, and put his hands upon him, he asked him if he saw ought. And he looked up, and said, I see men as trees, walking. After that he put his hands again upon his eyes, and made him look up : and he was restored, and saw every man clearly " (*Mark* viii. 22–25).

13. PERSECUTED AND SLANDERED.

"God is jealous, and the Lord revenges," said the prophet ; and he claims vengeance to himself as that which he only has a right to dispense, or could safely be trusted with. He is jealous of his people's good name and honour, though he bear long with their slanderers, and he speaks words of comfort, and strength, and sympathy for days of suffering and evil.

" Blessed are they which are persecuted for righteousness' sake : for theirs is the kingdom of heaven. Blessed are ye, when men shall revile you, and persecute you, and shall say all manner of evil against you falsely, for my sake. Rejoice, and be exceeding glad : for great is your reward in heaven : for so persecuted they the prophets which were before you " (*Matt.* v. 10–12).

" But and if ye suffer for righteousness' sake, happy are ye : and be not afraid of their terror, neither be troubled ; but sanctify the Lord God in your hearts : and be ready always to give an answer to every man that asketh you a reason of the hope that is in you with meekness and fear : having a good conscience ; that, whereas they speak evil of you, as of evil doers, they may be ashamed that falsely accuse your good conversation in Christ. For it is better, if the will of God be so, that ye suffer for well doing, than for evil doing " (1 *Pet.* iii. 14–17).

"So that we ourselves glory in you in the churches of God for your patience and faith in all your persecutions and tribulations that ye endure: which is a manifest token of the righteous judgment of God, that ye may be counted worthy of the kingdom of God, for which ye also suffer: seeing it is a righteous thing with God to recompense tribulation to them that trouble you; and to you who are troubled rest with us, when the Lord Jesus shall be revealed from heaven with his mighty angels" (2 *Thess.* i. 4–7).

" For this is thankworthy, if a man for conscience toward God endure grief, suffering wrongfully. For what glory is it, if, when ye be buffeted for your faults, ye shall take it patiently? but if, when ye do well, and suffer for it, ye take it patiently, this is acceptable with God" (1 *Pet.* ii. 19, 20).

" But call to remembrance the former days, in which, after ye were illuminated, ye endured a great fight of afflictions; partly, whilst ye were made a gazing-stock both by reproaches and afflictions; and partly, whilst ye became companions of them that were so used. For ye had compassion of me in my bonds, and took joyfully the spoiling of your goods, knowing in yourselves that ye have in heaven a better and an enduring substance. Cast not away therefore your confidence, which hath great recompence of reward" (*Heb.* x. 32–35).

" Hear the word of the Lord, ye that tremble at his word; Your brethren that hated you, that cast you out for my name's sake, said, Let the Lord be glorified: but he shall appear to your joy, and they shall be ashamed" (*Isa.* lxvi. 5).

14. THE CONQUEROR.

It is to *warfare* that we are called, and it is expected of us that we war a good warfare. It is the battle of faith. It is the victory of faith. For this is the victory that overcometh the world, even our faith. Promises and rewards to the conqueror, "to him that overcometh," are held forth by Him who has led the way in this warfare, and has shown us how to overcome.

" For whatsoever is born of God overcometh the world : and this is the victory that overcometh the world, even our faith. Who is he that overcometh the world, but he that believeth that Jesus is the Son of God?" (1 *John* v. 4, 5.)

" To him that overcometh will I give to eat of the tree of life, which is in the midst of the paradise of God " (*Rev.* ii. 7).

" He that overcometh shall not be hurt of the second death " (*Rev.* ii. 11).

" To him that overcometh will I give to eat of the hidden manna, and will give him a white stone, and in the stone a new name written, which no man knoweth saving he that receiveth it " (*Rev.* ii. 17).

" He that overcometh, and keepeth my works unto the end, to him will I give power over the nations " (*Rev.* ii. 26).

" He that overcometh, the same shall be clothed in white raiment; and I will not blot out his name out of the book of life, but I will confess his name before my Father, and before his angels " (*Rev.* iii. 5).

" Him that overcometh will I make a pillar in the temple of my God, and he shall go no more out: and I will write upon him the name of my God, and the name of the city of my God, which is new Jerusalem, which cometh down out of heaven from my God: and I will write upon him my new name " (*Rev.* iii. 12).

" To him that overcometh will I grant to sit with me in my throne, even as I also overcame, and am set down with my Father in his throne " (*Rev.* iii. 21).

" He that overcometh shall inherit all things; and I will be his God, and he shall be my son " (*Rev.* xxi. 7).

Besides these cases and classes which we have thus indicated, there are many others which we can hardly do more than name. The completion of the catalogue, and the exhaustion of the texts under each head, would require a very large volume. A specimen will suffice. It will at least put our readers on the track, and give them some help in filling up the list.

Hearing. " Blessed is the man that heareth me" (*Prov.* viii. 34). " Blessed are they that hear the word of God " (*Luke* xi. 28).

Doing. " If ye know these things, happy are ye if ye do them" (*John* xiii. 17). " He that doeth these things shall never be moved" (*Ps.* xv. 5).

Reading. " Blessed is he that readeth" (*Rev.* i. 3).

Keeping. " Blessed is he that keepeth the sayings of the prophecy of this book" (*Rev.* xxii. 7).

Working. " Blessed are they that sow beside all waters" (*Isa.* xxxii. 20). " Let us not be weary in well doing: for in due season we shall reap, if we faint not" (*Gal.* vi. 9).

Fearing. " Happy is the man that feareth alway" (*Prov.* xxviii. 14). " There is no want to them that fear him" (*Ps.* xxxiv. 9).

Trusting. " He that trusteth in the Lord, mercy shall compass him about " (*Ps.* xxxii. 10). " Blessed is the man that trusteth in Him " (*Ps.* xxxiv. 8).

Loving. "I love them that love me" (*Prov.* viii. 17). " He that loveth me shall be loved of my Father " (*John* xiv. 21).

Following. " He that followeth me shall not walk in darkness" (*John* viii. 12). "Verily I say unto you, that ye which have followed me, in the regeneration when the Son of man shall sit on the throne of his glory, ye also shall sit upon twelve thrones, judging the twelve tribes of Israel " (*Matt.* xix. 28).

Hoping. " We are saved by hope " (*Rom.* viii. 24). " Happy is he whose hope is in the Lord his God " (*Ps.* cxlvi. 5).

Pitying. " He that hath pity upon the poor lendeth to the Lord" (*Prov.* xix. 17). " Blessed are the merciful " (*Matt.* v. 7).

Praying. " Whatsoever ye shall ask in prayer, believing, ye shall receive" (*Matt.* xxi. 22). " Ask, and ye shall receive " (*John* xvi. 24).

Almsgiving. " Thy prayers and thine alms are come up for a memorial before God " (*Acts* x. 4).

Giving. " There is that scattereth, and yet increaseth " (*Prov.* xi. 24). " Give, and it shall be given unto you" (*Luke* vi. 38). " He that soweth sparingly shall reap also sparingly ; and he that soweth bountifully shall reap also bountifully " (2 *Cor.* ix. 6). " The liberal deviseth liberal things; and by liberal things shall he stand " (*Isa.* xxxii. 8).

Confessing. " Whosoever shall confess me before men, him will I confess before my Father which is in heaven " (*Matt.* x. 32).

Believing. " By faith ye stand " (2 *Cor.* i. 24). " He that believeth in me, though he were dead, yet shall he live " (*John* xi. 25). " All that believe are justified from all things " (*Acts* xiii. 39).

Watching. " Blessed are those servants whom the Lord when he cometh shall find watching " (*Luke* xii. 37). " Blessed is he that watcheth " (*Rev.* xvi. 15).

As all these foregoing promises came out from God, so do they return to him from whom they came; and we, through them, get more fully into the mind and heart of him who has written them for us. As all these promises are sealed in and by Christ, who is "the Amen, the faithful and true witness," so do they all reveal him, both in his grace and glory; each one a declaration of him whose name is "the Christ of God," a fragment of his fulness; a special aspect of his gospel.

They are the true sayings of God; the words of him who cannot lie. Heaven and earth may pass away, but not one jot or tittle of these can fail.

We rest on these with certainty; for he who spoke them is the Spirit of truth; and he did not speak at random, as men do; he meant what he said, in every one of them. We need not fear to trust them too much. Our danger lies in trusting them too little, and so doing injustice to the faithfulness and love of God.

As Joshua said to Israel, so does he say to us: "Ye know in all your hearts and in all your souls, that not one thing hath failed of all the good things which the Lord your God spake concerning you; all are come to pass unto you, and not one thing hath failed thereof" (Josh. xxiii. 14). To this the church of past ages has borne full testimony; and to this each saint, as he passes on in his pilgrimage to the kingdom, bears witness still. Man's words fail, God's cannot. Human promises may be broken, Divine promises stand; and he who builds on these promises stands also, immovable as the word and will of God.

Earth's history is full of broken promises, and its ground strewed with violated oaths. Man has not been true to his fellow man. He often speaks and writes words that he has neither the power nor the intention of fulfilling.

The church's history is the reverse of all this. No broken promises lie scattered along its path. God has kept faith with his saints, and will keep it to the end. No jot nor tittle shall fail, for he is not a man that he should lie. He has never wronged us by one broken promise; let us not wrong him by distrust or suspicion. He has been true to us, let us be true to him.

His sayings are faithful, and he himself is TRUTH.